Southern Africa

MANAGING EDITORS
Amy Bauman
Barbara J. Behm

CONTENT EDITORS
Amanda Barrickman
James I. Clark
Patricia Lantier
Charles P. Milne, Jr.
Katherine C. Noonan
Christine Snyder
Gary Turbak
William M. Vogt
Denise A. Wenger
Harold L. Willis
John Wolf

ASSISTANT EDITORS
Ann Angel
Michelle Dambeck
Barbara Murray
Renee Prink
Andrea J. Schneider

INDEXER
James I. Clark

ART/PRODUCTION
Suzanne Beck, Art Director
Andrew Rupniewski, Production Manager
Eileen Rickey, Typesetter

Library of Congress Number: 88-18337

2 3 4 5 6 7 8 9 0   97 96 95 94 93 92

Library of Congress Cataloging-in-Publication Data

Daturi, Augusta, 1954-
  [Africa meridionale English]
  Southern Africa / Augusta Daturi, Carlo Violani.

  — (World nature encyclopedia)
  Translation of: Africa meridionale
  Includes index.
  Summary: Describes the plant and animal life of southern
Africa and its interaction with the environment.
    1. Ecology—Africa, Southern—Juvenile literature. 2. Biotic
communities—Africa, Southern—Juvenile literature.
  [1. Ecology—Africa, Southern. 2. Africa, Southern.]
  I. Violani, Carlo, 1946-. II. Title. III. Series: Natura nel
mondo. English.
QH195.A323D3713 1988 574.5'264'096—dc19 88-18416
ISBN 0-8172-3325-3

Cover Photo: Anthony Bannister—Animals Animals

WORLD NATURE ENCYCLOPEDIA

Southern Africa

Augusta Daturi
Carlo Violani

RAINTREE
STECK-VAUGHN
L I B R A R Y

Austin, Texas

CONTENTS

INTRODUCTION

Thinking about Africa brings to mind boundless prairies inhabited by large herds of grazing and browsing animals, great rivers crossing tropical forests, and vast and treacherous deserts. In these exotic landscapes, death may be around the corner in the form of a poisonous snake, a drought, or a merciless sun.

However, there is more to Africa than this. In the north, the narrow Mediterranean strip facing Europe and the Middle East resembles its neighbors in climate and flora and fauna (plants and animals). In the south, there is another climatic strip having a subtropical and temperate climate very similar to that of Mediterranean Africa. Many of the plants that originated in this southern region have spread to the Mediterranean area, where they are now very common. Toward the north, the Mediterranean climatic strip of Southern Africa makes a gradual transition to mountains, deserts, and savannas (tropical or subtropical grasslands characterized by scattered trees and drought-resistant

undergrowth). There are, however, no sudden changes, as is the case of the Mediterranean climatic strip of northern Africa, which borders the Sahara Desert. The Kalahari Desert of southern Africa is not as vast and hostile as the Sahara.

There are several islands east of the southern African coast. Most of them are small, with the exception of Madagascar. These islands, though belonging to Africa geographically, have little in common with the mainland from a biological and environmental standpoint.

Their origin links them partly to Asia and partly to primeval lands which have vanished long ago. Madagascar and the other islands are inhabited by lemurs (a nocturnal animal that is active at night), black parrots, giant tortoises, the singing thrush bird, elephant birds, and were the home of the now-extinct dodo bird. The coelacanth fish lives in the waters of Madagascar.

SOUTHERN AFRICA

Geology and Topography

Southern Africa includes all of Africa south of the seventeenth parallel. This approximate limit coincides more exactly with a line marked by two rivers: the Cunene in the west and the Zambezi in the east. The boundary line between these rivers is formed by the southern borders of Angola and Zambia.

From a geological standpoint, southern Africa is made up of some of the oldest rock formations ever recorded, as well as rocks of more recent origin. The lower layer is formed by an ancient and stable portion of the earth's crust.

The physical features of southern Africa include a series of highlands, valleys and mountains. These mountains are sometimes grouped to form spectacular massifs, or principal mountain masses, which at times stand out as solitary structures in the midst of vast flatlands. Three principal features can be distinguished.

The interior regions are occupied by a vast plateau with an average elevation of about 4,000 feet (1,200 meters). This plateau is the southern part of the great African plateau, which extends north all the way to the Sahara Desert. Its outer reaches look like a large plain with small hills and flat areas. A few mountain peaks appear in this plateau, which is carved by shallow river valleys. Toward the interior is the Kalahari Basin. The red-gray sands of the soil allow the scarce rainfall to penetrate easily, which gives the Kalahari a desert appearance.

The outer limit of the highland is marked by a spectacular, steep slope. This appears as a continuous wall which varies considerably along its entire length according to the various rock formations. In the areas where it is formed by resistant quartz and lava rocks it maintains a steep profile. Otherwise, where more compact and uniform rocks appear, such as the granites and schists, the hill slopes gently. This slope is more impressive along the great wall of the Drakensberg Mountains in Natal. Many of the highest peaks of southern Africa can be found in this region, some of which are close to 9,800 feet (3,000 m) in elevation.

Between the great slope and the coast lie the "marginal regions" with widths varying between 37 and 150 miles (60 and 240 kilometers). The eastern part of these lands was formed after the gradual receding of the slope toward the interior, which was caused by the erosion of the rivers flowing into the Indian Ocean.

This central area includes the Great Karroo Basin in

Preceding pages: One of the numerous and lonely beaches along the South African coast.

Opposite page: Landscape of Natal's Zululand.

Heading from the west coast of southern Africa toward the east, environments gradually become more humid. The desert is followed by a semi-desert area, the Karroo, then the savanna, and finally the forest along the east coast. In the southernmost region is the peculiar fynbos.

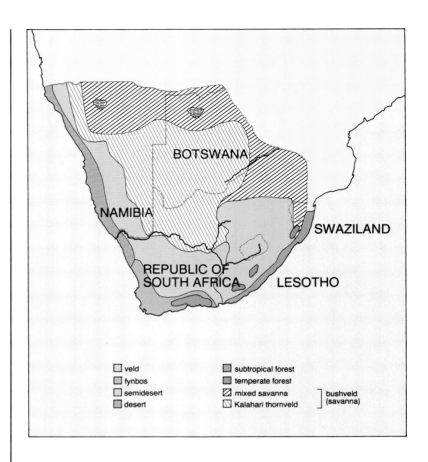

☐ veld	◻ subtropical forest
☐ fynbos	◻ temperate forest
☐ semidesert	▨ mixed savanna
☐ desert	◹ Kalahari thornveld

] bushveld (savanna)

the north and a headland (land jutting into the sea).

The Great Karroo Basin, which lies at an altitude between 2,100 and 3,000 feet (650 to 900 m), is an arid land. In the past, it was drained by rivers which have since carved spectacular canyons. The Great Karroo is rather flat in the south, while in the north it is characterized by numerous mesas (high plateaus).

These majestic, isolated mountains have steep slopes and flat summits. Heading westward, the marginal regions become a thin band of very dry lands near the coast. This area is occupied by the typical sand desert.

Climate

The climate of southern Africa is primarily influenced by the geographic position of the land. The ocean, which surrounds this land on three sides, and the high internal plateau are important climatic factors. This territory is also surrounded by an area where high-pressure conditions pre-

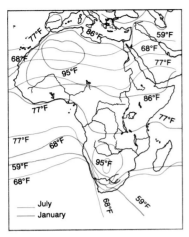

This map shows African temperatures.

vail, and where cloud formation does not occur. Therefore, precipitation is rare and the climate is generally dry.

The Atlantic and Indian oceans bordering the coastline of southern Africa have very different features. The waters of the Atlantic Ocean are colder than the waters of the Indian Ocean. The cold Benguela current of the Atlantic Ocean and the warm Aghulas current of the Indian Ocean are responsible for the difference in water temperature.

The influence of the oceans also affects the precipitation. Along the east coast warmer air masses prevail which, due to their natural instability, carry abundant rainfall. These air masses coming from the Indian Ocean are a major source of water for most of the land. However, they lose part of their moisture while moving west. For this reason, precipitation becomes less and less as the air masses move toward the west coast.

The great plateau, which rises in the interior of southern Africa, is responsible for the generally lower average temperature in relation to other areas of the world located at the same latitude but at lower elevations.

In most of the land, rain is prevalent during the Southern Hemisphere's summer season, from January to March. A very dry climate characterizes the winter. A wetter climate prevails only in a very limited area along the southwestern and western coast of Capetown Province. This region has a Mediterranean type climate with abundant winter rainfalls. Summers are hot and cloudless, but rather windy. Between these two regions lies a third intermediate region. In the intermediate region, rainfall is distributed throughout the year with two peaks, one in the spring and the other in the fall. Significant changes in rainfall occur annually, usually tending toward the dry side. Long periods of persistent drought occur, sometimes lasting several years. Droughts are usually followed by periods of great floods. In particular, these floods affect areas which normally receive summer rainfall.

The distribution of various types of vegetation is related to climatic patterns. The climate varies from tropical in the north to temperate in the south, and from a high altitude climate in the mountains to a Mediterranean climate in the extreme western part of the continent.

An Overview from the Desert to the Forests

Traveling from the western coast of southern Africa toward the east, there is a series of different types of plant

This peculiar finger-shaped rock lies 62 miles (100 km) southwest of Outjo in Namibia. It is called the "Fingerklip."

and animal communities. These communities are related to the particular geographical and environmental features of the area.

The coastal desert, which extends along the Namibian coast up to the lower valley of the Orange River, gradually reaches a semi-desert area. The Great Karroo Basin, which occupies a large portion of Cape Province, is typical of this semi-desert area. Toward the east several types of savannas (called bushveld) replace this semi-arid area. The western part of the savanna is more open and characterizes the so-called Kalahari thornveld. This area is marked by low, thorny bushes and sparse, grassy vegetation. The eastern part, in contrast, is characterized by thicker vegetation, with high-trunk trees, low underbrush, and grass.

This vegetation gradually gives way to a mixed savanna

12

with evergreen and deciduous trees (those which shed their leaves in autumn). Further south, the interior is occupied by prairies of a temperate type (veld), somewhat affected by repeated droughts and winter frost. These regions, which are covered by different types of grasses, generally lack trees.

Toward the Cape peninsula in the southwest, and partly in the extreme south, one encounters the fynbos (fine bush), an area of shrubby, mostly evergreen plants. In this region, the Mediterranean, type of climate, with rainy winters and dry summers, affects the survival of the vegetation of the Cape area.

Following the coastline (which moves toward the east from the fynbos) is a thin strip of temperate and subtropical forest.

THE NAMIB DESERT

A true desert environment is found in southern Africa. Starting from the western coast, the desert occupies a relatively limited area. It is a band from 9 to 78 miles (15 to 125 km) wide which reaches the lower valley of the Orange River in the east.

Vegetation

The landscape of this region is typical of a sandy desert with dunes and low scattered vegetation and shrubs. This is the environment of the so-called succulent plants (with juicy, fleshy tissues) as well as others.

Here, the vegetation had to evolve and adapt in order to survive and thrive in the hostile desert environment. The vegetation acquires its most typical aspect in the Namib Desert. Precipitation is usually very rare, from 2 to 5 inches (50 to 125 millimeters) per year. In certain years it does not rain at all. For this reason, local plants have become specialized in accumulating moisture and in defending themselves against high water losses. Certain plants have reduced their leaf surface in order to limit water evaporation and increase cooling. The sea fig plant has adapted its leaves into structures for gathering water.

The lilies of the Ammocharis genus store vital fluids in their large underground bulbs. Several types of ephemeral plants (plants that grow flowers and die in a few days) grow in the desert following the rare thunderstorms.

Seeds that are dormant during the dry period germinate as soon as the moisture from the rain is absorbed. An explosive blooming then takes place. Certain desert areas become covered with the yellow, white, and orange flowers of many different plants. Within a few weeks these plants die, but only after they have produced new seeds which will ensure the continuation of the cycle.

The cucurbit, a plant which produces melonlike fruits, has probably played an important role in the survival of humans in the Namib Desert. Its extremely long and twisted roots penetrate deeply into the sand until they reach the water table. On the surface, the plant has evolved into a smaller size to minimize its water loss caused by evaporation. Instead of leaves it has sharp, green thorns. The fruit is a large melon with a very hard shell. The juicy pulp on the inside can be used as food.

The most picturesque juicy plants of this dry area are the aloes (of the lily family), of which the kokerboom is the most typical. At times the kokerboom, which was disco-

Opposite page: The Namib Desert has a gravelly appearance. The typical sand dunes are found further south.

15

The kokerboom, with its unique shape, may reach a height of 30 feet (9 m). It is capable of withstanding long periods of drought by storing water in its tissues. Its branches have been used by the Bushmen for making arrow holders, while the trunk was used in the construction of their huts.

vered in 1685 by Dutch explorers, resembles a candelabrum. It can grow as high as 30 feet (9 m). It is a very slow-growing plant with a smooth bark, grayish green leaves, and yellow flowers. This plant can withstand the harshest conditions by storing water in the tissues within its trunk.

The welwitschia of the Namib Desert (named after the Austrian botanist Friedrich Welwitsch who discovered it in Angola) is one of the strangest plants ever discovered. This strange plant is believed to have a life span of 1,000 years. During this long life cycle it produces only two leaves which are 10 feet (3 m) long and grow directly out of a low, large trunk over 3 feet wide (1 m). Their tops have a frayed and twisted appearance due to the continuous effect of the sand and the heat of the desert. It appears that these plants

The unique welwitschia plant has primitive features and can live for one thousand years. It produces only two leaves that grow directly from a large and low stem.

contain millions of pores which close during daylight hours in order to reduce water loss. As the air cools the pores reopen and absorb moisture from the night fog.

Animal Life

There are even animals that thrive in the desert, though at first glance this environment seems quite barren.

Many biologists have described the Namib Desert as one of the most fascinating ecosystems of our planet. This is because the food chain of this environment is similar to that of the marine environment. The edible organic matter (debris) blown by the wind on the sand dunes may be compared to plankton (microscopic plant and animal organisms that float in water). Here the prime consumers that feed on the debris of the desert are the insects. The secondary consumers are the predators which feed on the insects and on other small animals.

The scorpions of this desert are known for their small pincers, or claws, in the front limbs and by a long abdomen ending with a powerful, poisonous stinger. These animals flourish especially in hot, arid conditions. There are known instances of scorpions having gone without food for twelve months and surviving with no apparent harm.

Another unique multi-legged animal of the desert is the so-called dancing-white-lady, a spider which burrows tunnels in the sand and covers them with silk threads. This spider stalks its prey at night from its hideout. Occasionally, the prey is larger than the spider, as in the case of desert crickets and other insects.

The unusual name of this animal derives from its habit of standing on its legs in an aggressive manner when threatened. It can also roll down the slopes of dunes by folding its legs into the form of a small white wheel.

The uncontested leaders, as far as desert adaptation is concerned, are numerous species of insects. The ants of the Camponothus genus live in active colonies with as many as twenty thousand members. These ants are almost always found at the bottom of sandy dunes where they search the scattered clusters of grasses for the main source of their food, the sugary liquid secreted by the cochineal insects (bright red insects which usually live on cacti). This aggressive ant often attacks any creature that might intrude into its territory with small discharges of acid (formic acid). It is even aggressive toward ants belonging to other colonies. Some entomologists (scientists who study insects) have dis-

Above: Ants of the *Camponothus* genus.

Opposite page: Some inhabitants of the desert are pictured. The flat-lizard is common in dry environments. It has a flat body for absorbing the maximum heat from the sun and rocks necessary to regulate its body functions. A viper *(above)* and a dwarf puff adder *(below)* bury themselves in the sand with S-shaped side movements. A desert beetle digs trenches in the sand in order to collect as much water as possible. The barking gecko and the webbed gecko (bottom) are two other animals of the desert that display unique behavioral patterns.

covered that in one area of the Namib Desert up to eleven different species of ants can be identified. They are presently studying the problem of the co-existence, or living together of these species, especially in view of the limited food resources available.

Environmental Problems

The water supply is a pressing problem for all living desert organisms. The breeze coming from the west, after being cooled by the Benguela current, reaches the desert interior in the form of a fog. In ideal conditions the fog condenses in minute drops on the sand, the vegetation, and the animals.

Consequently, many insects have evolved certain behaviors and particular ways for collecting the moisture essential for their metabolism (physical and chemical processes for maintaining life.) For example, certain beetles bury themselves under the sand until sunset, when they come out in search of edible debris. They can easily be spotted in the foggy morning as they dig narrow trenches up

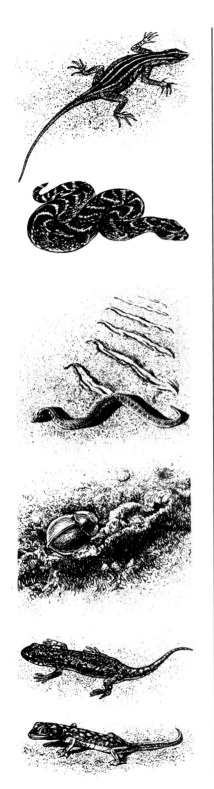

to 3 feet (1 m) long in the moist sand. The beetles build small ridges on the sides of these trenches, from which they are able to extract small quantities of drinking water. They wait for the moisture to condense in small, drinkable drops at the bottom of these trenches.

Another type of beetle has been described as a sort of living water condenser. On foggy mornings, this beetle lays upside down on top of a dune, with its abdomen raised vertically toward the wind direction. Here it waits for the fog droplets to condense on its abdomen and flow toward its mouth. In this way the insect is able to drink.

There are also numerous desert reptiles. The puff adder viper and the small horned adder are dangerously poisonous snakes. Both species can move quickly by writhing in S-shaped curves. They can hide in the sand by burying themselves in a few seconds.

At sunset, a chorus of sounds resembling the screeching of cicadas fills the dunes. This noise comes from the barking geckos, a type of lizard which lives in shelters burrowed beneath the desert sand. At night the noisy activity of the geckos dies down as they leave their shelters in search of termites, ants, and beetles, their preferred foods.

Another species of gecko found in the Namib Desert is the webbed gecko. This is a nocturnal insect-eater with webbed toes. By using its toes as a shovel, this lizard can dig a shelter in the sand. Its four unique legs enable it to stand on the uneven terrain of the desert.

The sand grouses are a group of birds that are typical of these dry environments. They originated in Europe and are distantly related to pigeons. They somewhat resemble partridges. The sand grouses feed on seeds and insects and drink water twice a day. They are definitely social animals, as they gather in the morning or evening in great flocks near water holes that may be located many miles from their own territory. Water is carried to their young in a peculiar way. While drinking, the male soaks its belly feathers with water. Upon returning to the nest, the young drink the drops from the wet feathers. If necessary, even the female cooperates in carrying water to the nest. There has been an adaptation of the structure of the feathers in the belly of both sexes.

The internal surface of the feathers is full of microscopic threads or fibers which are capable of soaking and holding considerable quantities of water. The location of these feathers in an unexposed part of the body prevents the immediate evaporation of the water that is being carried.

Above: The sandgrouse prefers a dry environment with scattered vegetation. In the morning and at sunset, groups gather by the hundreds and sometimes thousands near water holes.

Opposite page, above: The Tatera (above) and Gerbillurus (below) are rodents that have adapted to dry, desert lands. They dig simple dens and are active at night.

Opposite page, below: The oryx feeds on scarce desert vegetation. When water is not available it satisfies its thirst with fruits and succulent plants.

Groups of ostriches also inhabit this vast desert. Many ostrich species have descended from hybrid ostriches that were introduced to the wild. The hybrid ostriches were once raised on farms for their ornamental feathers. These huge, flightless birds can make long migrations in search of food. They feed primarily on seeds, flowers, and the highly nutritious leaves found among the scattered vegetation of the desert.

Another example of behavioral adaptation to such a hostile environment is offered by small rodents called gerbils. Gerbils are similar to mice and have elongated rear legs and large eyes suited for night vision. They dig holes in which an entire family lives. They feed on substances with low water content, such as seeds and insects, since their water requirement is relatively small.

The desert mole is a strange little insect-eater, which is active mostly at night. Like the European mole, it digs winding tunnels under the sand down to a depth of 1 foot (30 centimeters) while searching for insects, spiders, and small reptiles.

Gazelles, Antelope, and Zebras

The gemsbok gazelle displays the most elegant coat of hair of all the desert ruminants (animals that chew cud, i.e., food regurgitated from the stomach to the mouth). Its coat is made up of contrasting colors. In the dark gray area of its body, the black and white shadows of the legs stand out along with the striking white and black mask of its snout. This animal has straight and sharp horns, which differ somewhat in the male and the female. These horns are an excellent weapon against large predators, including humans. Several herds of these gazelles also live in other southern African environments such as the savanna and the steppe. The gazelles inhabiting the desert and the dry areas are nomadic, meaning that they move from place to place in search of food, water, and grazing land. Their movements follow the rainfall. In the desert the gemsbok is able to survive quite well by feeding on scarce vegetation, including plants with leathery leaves, wild melons, and roots and bulbs, which it digs out with its front hooves. If the gazelle is unable to find a water hole for drinking, it digs in the soil in search of a spring. It may also try to quench its thirst by eating succulent plants or by lapping dew. At times the gazelles form herds of thirty to two hundred animals.

The Hartmann zebra *(top)* lives under protection in the Namib National Park in the Naukluft Mountains. A similar subspecies, the extremely rare mountain zebra *(bottom)*, has been brought back from almost certain extinction through a clever breeding program. It has been reintroduced into its original habitat starting from a few original survivors. The largest herd (about two hundred animals) can be found today in the Mountain Zebra National Park near Cradock in Cape Province.

Their ability to see, smell, and hear is excellent. This explains why gazelles are able to detect persons moving, or hear the engines of motor vehicles and helicopters, even at distances of up to three-fourths of a mile (about 1 km). Upon hearing these noises, the gazelles immediately flee.

The main enemies of the gazelle (after humans, who are responsible for their partial disappearance in many areas of southern Africa) are the cheetah, the leopard, and the lion. Large fragments of a gazelle's sharp horns were once discovered in the body of a dying lioness. Smaller predators, such as hyenas and jackals generally attack the young gazelles, which are, however, fiercely defended by their mother.

Other typical herbivores, or plant-eaters, which can be found in the Namib Desert are the springbok or jumping antelopes. These animals are well known for the massive migrations of the last century, consisting of hundreds of

The springbok was once a common sight. In the last 150 years, however, its population has been drastically reduced by extensive hunting. Now it has been reintroduced into its natural habitat. Its latin name *Antidorcas marsupialis* refers to a skin pocket along its back. This pocket is full of skin glands and long hair which spread like a fan when the animal is alarmed. This feature serves as a warning signal to the herd. Once the alarm is given, the entire group begins to flee.

thousands of animals.

Near the Namib Desert, specifically in the Naukluft Mountains, live a group of rare Hartmann zebras. These zebras have adapted quite well to the arid environment. They represent a subspecies of zebra which has been reduced to a few thousand animals in the last few years. The Hartmann zebra resembles the extremely rare mountain zebra except for its size and its narrower black stripes. In 1960, Namibia acquired the Naukluft territory and later purchased several farms from which the Namib Park was formed. The park was established to provide adequate space for the migratory movements of this rare animal from the mountains to the western plains.

THE KARROO, THE SAVANNA, THE VELD

Crossing the arid coastal Namib Desert and heading toward the interior, the aspect of the country gradually changes until it gives way to the semi-arid vegetation of the Karroo. The word Karroo, adopted by the Dutch pioneers, is derived from an ancient Hottentot word appropriately meaning arid or sterile. The Hottentots are native people of southern Africa.

Vegetation of the Karroo

Low, scattered shrubs of a woody consistency not more than two feet (60 cm) high grow in the Karroo. These shrubs are perennial, meaning they live for more than one year. Along with these shrubs are succulent plants (plants having fleshy tissues, i.e., cacti) and grasses of a modest height.

Rainfall is rare and irregular, falling at an annual rate of 5 to 15 inches (125 to 365 mm). For this reason local plants have been able to develop several mechanisms for retaining as much water as possible in their systems. Many plants have root systems that have developed horizontally and grow to only a small depth in the ground. Other plants have very small leaves to prevent excessive evaporation.

A typical example of the Karroo vegetation can be seen in the Karroo National Park. Here, in a series of mountains, plains, mesas, and canyons, botanists have been able to identify different plant families corresponding to different altitudes.

In the plains, the grasses are the most common vegetation, intermingled with shrubs, of which the Karroo acacia is typical. This plant, widely scattered in southern Africa, acquires a bushy appearance when appearing in the semi-desert environment. Its flowers, enclosed in golden and very fragrant heads, play an important ecological role because they attract swarms of pollinating insects.

In addition, numerous species of spurges have adapted quite well to this arid environment. These plants are able to store a considerable quantity of water in their enlarged stems and their leaves have evolved into sharp thorns.

On the mountain slopes, grasses and grayish green rhinoceros shrubs mark the areas that have cooler climates, where rainfalls are more frequent.

Animals of the Karroo

The rocky plains of the Karroo are an ideal habitat for several antelope, the most common being the steinbok. The steinbok is a small ruminant, 18 to 20 inches (45 to 50 cm)

Opposite page: The steinbok also inhabits areas outside the Karroo. It is commonly seen in the savanna and in other open areas with scattered vegetation. It can disappear from the line of sight of predators in a unique way. Following a fast pursuit, the steinbok hides by lowering its head among the vegetation, or it can hide in the den of an aardvark. This animal is usually a loner except during the mating season, when it lives in pairs. Both sexes mark their territory by rubbing their facial glands on the vegetation.

A male and female Karroo bustard *(above)*, the black-eared skylark *(center, male and female)* and the Karroo honey guide *(below)*. These three species are primarily found in the Karroo. They prefer dry environments where the scattered vegetation consists mainly of bushes.

tall at the shoulders. Only the male of this species has horns. The steinbok is active during the day and on nights with a full moon. Other herbivores—some of which were later introduced into the Karroo National Park—are the rare mountain zebra, the oribi, the springbok, and the white-tail wildebeest (a type of antelope).

The wildebeest, practically extinct in the wild, has been reintroduced in certain reserves located in the middle of its ancient habitat. The caracal, a wild cat similar to the European lynx, is a typical predator of the plains, the savannas, and the semi-arid areas. This carnivore, or meat-eater, has a coat of a uniform color and black, tufted ears. In its natural habitat it preys on animals of any size, from rodents to small antelope. The caracal also preys on flying birds, which it seizes by jumping from a branch or a rock.

The birds of the semidesert areas have feathers with pale and drab colors. A few species of bustards are quite common in this environment. One of them, the Karroo bustard, can be spotted in pairs in arid areas with small shrubs. Several species of ground-feeding larks are found in these areas.

The Karroo chat is far more conspicuous. This is one of the most common singing birds of the thrush family in the Karroo. It usually sits on the tops of shrubs where it sings its "tirr-tit-tat-tut."

Numerous animals are found even in rocky environments such as mesas, mountain slopes, and canyons with overhanging cliffs. These animals have adapted well to these conditions. At first glance, the rock hyraxes (similar to rodents but more closely related to the hoofed mammals) resemble large European marmots (stocky, coarse-furred rodents having short legs and ears and bushy tails). Actually, zoologists have established a relationship between the hyrax and the elephant in view of the similarities of their teeth and joints. They feed on tufts of vegetation scattered in the crevices of rocks and lay in the sun for long periods of time, especially in the morning.

The hyrax lives in colonies which are always under the careful surveillance of "guards," who warn of possible danger by making a whistling sound. The hyrax has excellent sight. Furthermore, its eye structure allows the eye to turn directly toward the sun. This feature is extremely useful because it prevents attacks from large birds of prey flying directly overhead. The feet of the hyrax are padded and kept constantly moist by sweat glands.

The caracal (a type of lynx) is commonly found in most of Africa and in India. Because of its agility, it was once trained in Iran for hunting hares and birds.

Vegetation of the Savanna

The bushveld occupies a great part of the wooded areas of southern Africa. This term corresponds to our concept of the savanna, an area dominated by trees having high trunks. Acacia trees and West Indian almond trees constitute the typical vegetation of the South African savanna. The vegetation is rather scattered, with a developed layer of shrubs. The savanna gradually changes to an area with thicker vegetation, characterized by large trees and a less extensive layer of shrubs. The so-called miombo tree is the predominant tree of this environment.

The mixed savanna has the appearance of a dry, dense thicket. The landscape includes the gigantic baobab which reaches a height of about 82 feet (25 m) and a diameter of 33 feet (10 m). The trunk of many older baobab trees is occasionally torn by elephants, which like to eat its bark.

The marula tree is very common and widely scattered. It has a large, round canopy that reaches a height of 60 feet (18 m). This tree is very important to the animals of the savanna. Elephants, baboons, and several species of primates are fond of its meaty fruits, which fall on the ground. The wart hogs greedily chew its hard seeds, which are rich in oil and vitamins. The natives of Africa distill (extract) a

In its most dense state, the vegetation of the savanna is characterized by trees with high trunks and by a thick undergrowth. This is the so-called mixed savanna. This landscape blends slowly into a more open savanna, the Kalahari thornveld. This area features low, thorny bushes and rather scattered grasses. The two types of savanna are shown alongside each other in the illustration.

highly alcoholic beverage from these fruits. They also use the bark to make medicine for curing dysentery and malaria.

Another easily recognized tree is the mopane, which prevails in certain areas, reaching a height of up to 50 feet (15 m). Its leaves look like two joined triangular parts, very similar to the open wings of a butterfly. Due to their high nutritional value, the leaves and buds of the mopane are a favorite food for the elephants, who readily uproot entire plants.

The driest area of the savanna slowly turns into a more open type of savanna known as the thornveld. Here, several bushy, treelike types of acacia with large thorns predominate. Among these trees the giraffe acacia is the most noticeable, due to its height. The soil is mainly sand and it is often covered by a thin carpet of vegetation. This is in fact what most of the Kalahari Desert looks like. The Kalahari resembles a dry, thorny savanna rather than a sandy desert. The giraffe acacia has almost become a symbol of the Kalahari Desert with its colorful umbrella profile. This evergreen is covered with fragrant, yellow flowers enclosed in round tufts during the blossoming season (August to November).

Animals of the Savanna

The visitor who explores by jeep the savannas of the many national parks will be amazed by the abundance of large mammals and the variety of birds of different shapes and colors. Small groups of giraffes stick their necks out of the green canopies of the acacia trees. The giraffes chew the twigs and leaves of the acacias, rolling them toward the mouth with their tongues. At the same time, herds of elephants can be seen splashing themselves with sand and muddy water. In the hottest hours it is easy to spot rhinoceroses sheltering themselves in the shadows of trees. Rhinos are more active in the early morning or evening hours.

The favorite observation points for visitors are the drinking holes. In the evenings, several species of herbivores as well as flocks of guinea fowls can usually be spotted. Groups of wart hogs mingle with zebras and giraffes near

the water holes in the morning and in the afternoon. At night, or in the middle of the day, the wart hogs prefer to rest and protect themselves from the sun in shelters dug inside termite mounds or sometimes in the middle of shrubs.

The kudu is a majestic antelope 5 feet (1.5 m) high at the shoulder, whose male displays long spiral-shaped horns. The females live in groups with their young. The males can form herds of forty animals after the mating season.

The male nyala antelope is characterized by its smaller size, dark gray coat, and large spiral horns. The female (without horns) has a reddish coat with white stripes. The habitat of this antelope includes woody areas of the savanna near water and both flat and hilly areas. The waterbuck, or the kobo, is associated with a moist environment, where it drinks during the day. The horns of the male, which arch upward and toward the back, are marked by prominent rings.

By exploring the grassy plains and the open mopane woodlands, it is possible to spot the rare sassaby antelope. Both sexes display horns that resemble the lyre, a musical instrument. Long legs give the sassaby a fragile yet athletic appearance, and it is considered among the fastest of the African antelopes. Another antelope that travels in great herds is the gnu. During the rainy season the gnu herds number up to one thousand animals. If threatened, this animal becomes aggressive and can ward off even lions by creating a semicircle with herd members.

The Chapman zebra can also be found at drinking holes. It is one of the most abundant species and a favorite prey of lions. A favorite meal for the cheetah is the jumping antelope. This animal can accomplish remarkable migrations in herds numbering up to two or three thousand animals.

Sea jays can easily be seen above the thorny knots of the acacias. When these birds spot grasshoppers, scorpions, or beetles they fly close to the ground, where the blue colors of their wings and tail can be observed.

The playing falcon is one of the major predators and is well-known for its aerial acrobatics. The singing goshawk can often be seen perched motionless on the tallest trees. It prefers walking slowly, searching for lizards and large insects.

The majestic pace of the secretary bird is unmistakable among the grasses of the savanna. This bird extracts insects

Springbok, zebras, and wildebeest gather at a water hole. During the dry season the few remaining water holes are gathering places for all the animals of the savanna.

Because of its long and strong legs, the secretary bird is able to run quickly. It flies only when seriously threatened. Its nest, consisting of a conspicuous platform of twigs, is usually built on bushes or small acacia trees. The secretary bird feeds on insects, lizards, snakes, turtles, young birds, and all kinds of small animals.

and reptiles from their nests with its long legs, while shielding itself with its open wings.

When exploring these regions for the first time, enormous stacks of straw are often seen intertwined among the branches of large acacias. This is a common sight along the paths crossing the woodlands, even at the end of the red dunes of the Kalahari. These are the large nests of the weaverbird, which can sometimes reach a length of 13 feet (4 m). The weaverbird enters its egg incubation chamber through an opening to a passage in the lower side of the nest. The nests may be widened year after year and the empty chambers are often taken over by other species of

birds such as dwarf parrots and small falcons. On the roof of these weaver colonies one can find nests of owls. Quite often, poisonous snakes prey on these nests.

The Veld

A large part of eastern South Africa is occupied by vegetation typical of temperate prairies, known as the veld. Most of this region lacks trees. In large areas, however, the original prairie has undergone great changes brought about by overgrazing and agriculture. Little remains of the original prairie.

In this region, extensive farming of the land has greatly affected the white-tailed wildebeest. This animal was plentiful up to the early years of the last century. However, hunting, practiced on a large scale because of the precious meat and skin, almost led to the extinction of the species. Only two private farms have been able to restore part of the wildebeest population, which today thrives in several natural reserves.

Although not exclusive to the veld, certain burrowing mammals are rather common here. The suricate, a type of prairie dog, lives in small family groups inside underground tunnels. This animal bathes in the sun while standing in position outside its shelter.

Ground squirrels are active during the day and in the late afternoon outside their tunnels, which have many openings. It is easy to spot these rodents basking in the sun. They are always ready to disappear underground at the first sign of danger.

The birds of the veld, like those of other open spaces, do not display lively colors or conspicuous behavioral patterns. Such behavior could attract the unwanted attention of keen-sighted predators. Francolins, bustards, and many species of larks and wagtails are some of the birds that have adapted to this environment.

Even the crane is a common sight in the veld. It travels in pairs or small groups in search of insects and small reptiles. Its diet includes seeds, buds, and cereals. In spite of its popularity (it is the national bird of South Africa), the crane is not appreciated by farmers and is hunted down because of the damage it causes to their crops.

THE FYNBOS

At the southern extremity of Africa, between the mountains of the Cape and toward the coast, there is an unusual type of vegetation, unique in the world. This is the Cape vegetation, similar to a green blanket interrupted here and there by colorful spots. This vegetation covers the mountain slopes and almost reaches the ocean.

Vegetation of the Cape

Despite its limited distribution, the vegetation of the Cape is so unusual that it could be considered as a separate plant kingdom. This is justified by the great number of species present, which grow exclusively in this area.

The vegetation includes a variety of species, of which the so-called fynbos (Dutch for fine bush) is the most typical. The fynbos can be found in the small area of southern Africa affected by a typically Mediterranean climate. The fynbos is very similar to the Mediterranean thicket, and it consists of an assortment of shrubs with leathery evergreen leaves capable of sustaining long periods of summer drought.

The term fynbos was used by the first colonists in describing this strange vegetation, which lacked the grasses required for sustaining their herds of livestock. The fynbos consists of shrub-type vegetation with small leaves. This is an amazing and interesting environment from a botanical and ecological standpoint. The presence of beautiful plants and flowers contributes to the beauty of this landscape.

Generally, the vegetation is dominated by a few species of plants, many of them belonging to the restio family, which are perennial herbs with long tubular stems.

The fynbos is well known for its variety of plant species. Changes in vegetation can be easily noticed by moving just a few dozen yards within the same area, along slopes of a mountain or in a narrow valley. At least 2,600 different species of plants have been counted within an area of 181 square miles (470 sq. km) surrounding the Cape. Of these plants, 212 are native to the area. This represents the highest rate of native plant concentration in the world.

Certain native organisms confirm the existence of a micro-habitat inside a small territory. Other native organisms point instead to a very "young" vegetation, confirming a relatively recent evolution. This is especially true of the coastal areas, where the advancing or receding waterline of the Pleistocene period brought about the evolution of new life forms adaptable to the changing environment.

Opposite page: The fynbos as seen in the reserve of Kleinmond.

The restio grasses are always present in the fynbos. There are thirty species that belong to this group, all unique to the Southern Hemisphere. They are common especially in South Africa and Australia. They look like reeds, and their small flowers are held together in small spikes. Together they form low flower clusters.

The botanist is aware of differences between the mountain and the coastal fynbos, even if they may appear very similar at first glance.

In certain areas, the mountain fynbos is close to the ocean, although it is generally separated from the sea by the coastal plain. It does not have a uniform appearance because the soil, the humidity level, the altitude and the topography (physical features of a place or region) of the mountain slopes affect the type of vegetation and its development.

At the bottom of the mountains and in the lower lands, the silk-oak vegetation is most plentiful. This area reaches the altitude of 2,952 to 3,280 feet (900 to 1,000 m) along the shadowy slopes. The shrubs and trees of the silk-oak family are found at higher altitudes along the sunnier and warmer slopes. These plants reach a height of 8 feet (2.5 m) and more. Their appearance varies from round shrubs to that of small trees with wide leaves and a hairy, light blue surface. The fynbos becomes more complex in areas where the silk-oaks are well-developed. Here vegetation can be subdivided into several layers. The highest layer reaches a height

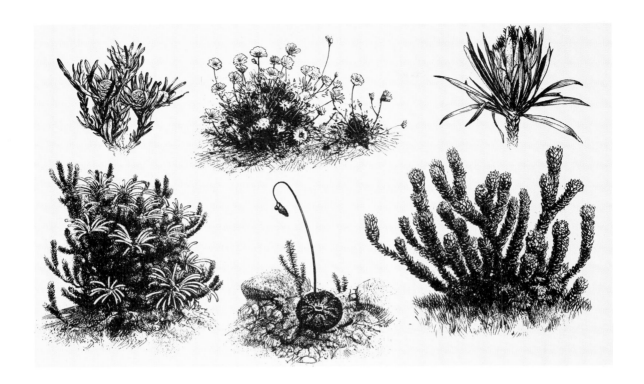

A few plants typical of the fynbos. *From left to right and from top to bottom:* the tea tree, *Augrabies* (genus), long-leaved silk-oak, heath, *Protea caliciflora* (a type of silk-oak), *Mimites hirtus.*

of 10 feet (3 m) and, in particularly favorable conditions, it can grow as tall as 20 feet (6 m). The lower level is, in contrast, very dense and entangled.

Climbing toward higher elevations the silk-oaks gradually become smaller and the vegetation acquires a simpler structure. The tall silk-oaks, restricted to the more sheltered areas, make room for the low bushes of the heath and restio families. These plants, characterized by narrow and rigid leaves, are no more than 3 feet (1 m) tall. The landscape acquires a bright-gray appearance and in certain seasons white, pink, and yellow specks appear as the heaths and mallows blossom.

There are never more than two layers of vegetation present in the same season. During the winter, snows and winds, which are often strong, can last for long periods. In places where the vegetation is more exposed to the winds, the tall bushes become scattered, or they may disappear altogether.

Several mountains in the Cape region are more than 8,860 feet (2,700 m) high. Above this altitude many plants have the appearance of typically alpine plants. Some form a carpet or are flattened among the boulders, similar to the dwarf juniper of the Northern Hemisphere. The mountain fynbos also include vegetation found along the riverbanks, torrents, or swamps, where the soil is soaked with water. In these areas a community of plants thriving on moisture develops, and when fires do not damage them, a forest typical of the temperate climates is formed.

Past the mountains and heading toward the interior, there is a small, well-defined area characterized by a rather dry environment. This is the area of the so-called arid fynbos which is found along the mountain slopes between

1,640 and 3,280 feet (500 and 1,000 m) in elevation, on granite soil.

This type of fynbos is so typical that it must be considered separately from the mountain fynbos. Here the scant rainfall makes the vegetation extremely simple and scattered. Heaths are most common, along with a few silk-oaks. The restios appear only in a few specific locations. Between the mountains and the ocean, where the coastal fynbos dominates, the vegetation changes again.

During the Quaternary period, the sea level was 558 feet (170 m) above the present level. The mountains of the Cape peninsula emerged like many islands. Since then, the appearance of the coast has undergone various changes. With the formation of the present coastline, the fynbos vegetation was able to spread to new lands. The scant rainfall and the presence of the ocean, which prevents extremes in temperature, have favored a rather open environment and the growth of shrubs that are 3 feet (1 m) tall. Restios and heaths are also common here. Grasses and other perennial plants are more abundant than in the mountain fynbos.

Fires and Fynbos

In the year 1497, the Portuguese explorer Vasco da Gama named the lands near the Cape of Good Hope the "Smoky Lands." He did so after witnessing large columns of smoke rising in the sky. Spontaneous combustion (the act of burning naturally, by some internal cause) is, even today, a very common event, particularly in the dry season. The first European settlers considered these fires real calamities. In the seventeenth century unauthorized fires were forbidden by the law. The offenders were punished with a whipping for the first offense and by death for the second.

The custom of burning small areas for the purpose of improving agriculture was common even before the arrival of the first European settlers. However, the effects of this practice were harmful to the Cape vegetation. Though the grasses were able to regenerate themselves quickly, the silk-oaks slowly began to disappear.

In the early 1800s, this practice alarmed many botanists because they believed that fires were real threats to the survival of native plants. Only recently has the role of fire been understood from an ecological standpoint. Fire is now accepted as an essential element for the survival of the fynbos. Under natural conditions, fires caused by lightning,

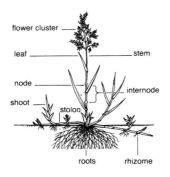

flower cluster

leaf

node

shoot

stolon

stem

internode

roots

rhizome

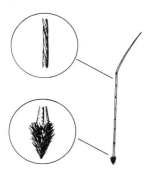

Above: Structure of a grass plant whose rhizomes, by reaching underground, allow the plant to survive in the event of fire.

Below: Stem structure and hair covering on a root tip. These features contribute to plant survival.

friction, or landslides following earthquakes, are rather frequent. Consequently, plant life evolved and adapted to the possibility of fires by adopting several strategies. Some plants (called geophytes) are able to regenerate through their underground organs (such as bulbs and tubers) which the fire cannot reach.

Other plants (called pyrophyles) are able to sprout again from the base of their stem once the fire is over. Still other plants are endowed with a thick bark that protects the buds. Finally, certain woody shrubs, though destroyed by fire, regenerate themselves through seeds which remain undamaged due to their heat-resistant capsules. Because of such devices, the vegetation is able to recover rather quickly after the apparent total destruction brought about by fire.

The first plants to rise again from the burned soil are the grasses and the restios. Blossoming species appear soon after. Plants with underground bulbs and tubers also appear, with truly amazing blossoms. These stupendous blossoms become poorer and less frequent until. a fire occurs again. Generally, in their first stages of regeneration, most of the fynbos plants reproduce themselves quickly.

The woody shrubs, which survive because of their heat-resistant seeds, are the most vulnerable plants. In fact, from the time when seeds sprout to the time when new plants produce seeds, five or six years may go by. Therefore, if within this period a new fire starts, the new generation will lose its chance of establishing itself. Fortunately, especially in regard to the silk-oaks and the heaths, seeds are not often destroyed by fire. In most cases, seeds are able to sprout only after receiving a heat stimulus from the fire itself.

Numerous examples confirm the effectiveness of these natural mechanisms. One of the most interesting examples concerns the *Serruria florida*, a silk-oak discovered for the first time in 1773. This plant was not seen again until 110 years later, when specimens were spotted in the mountains. This sensational discovery attracted much interest in the scientific world. Unfortunately, the scientists soon realized that this population was gradually shrinking. Therefore, starting from 1930, the plant was placed under protection.

A new survey carried out in 1962 showed that the plant had disappeared altogether from the original site. Only a few plants under poor conditions were found in a not-too-distant area. Efforts to remove a large number of

The heath with white flowers (or with very colorful flowers in other species) represents one of the essential elements of the fynbos.

weeds in that area did not help these silk-oaks, which continued to diminish. An accidental fire, however, was able to turn the tide of events. The seeds on the ground were partially burned and began to sprout. From that time on, the plant was able to reestablish itself successfully in that area.

The plant community of the fynbos is subject to continuous cycles. These cycles climax, or culminate, with a phase in which plants that reproduce themselves exclusively through seeds prevail. Among these, the tallest silk-

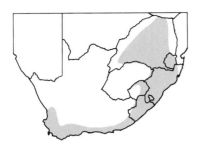

Distribution of the silk-oaks in South Africa.

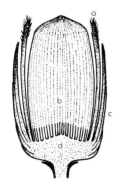

Cross section of a flower cluster of a silk-oak: a) internal bracts; b) group of single flowers; c) external bracts; d) receptacle.

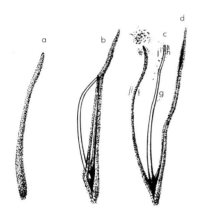

A silk-oak flower is shown in various stages of development: a) a flower in the bud; b) the flower style freeing itself of the external envelope (perianth); c) the open flower; d) the three sections of the perianth held together with their respective anthers; e) and f) the fourth segment of the perianth with anther; g) the style; h) the pollen dispenser.

oaks are able to dominate an area up to a period of twenty years. Nevertheless, before twenty years go by, another fire usually strikes. In this manner, from one fire to the other, the plant community changes continuously without ever reaching a period of stability. The action of fire is in balance with the vegetation. It represents an essential tool for the continuity of the species and for the start of a new cycle.

In theory, a fire should take place when the vegetation reaches a mature stage. For the silk-oaks in particular, the appropriate time would be when they become woody and dried out, and can no longer produce seeds. However, today it is always dangerous to wait until a fire starts spontaneously in a mature, dry, and highly flammable environment.

Spontaneous combustion of this type is difficult to bring under control and often poses a threat to populated areas. For this reason it is advisable to start a controlled fire in designated areas where the vegetation is sufficiently mature. Once the area has been designated, it is subdivided into sectors which are then burned separately. It is not possible to establish in advance the frequency with which fires should be started. This depends on specific local conditions. The average time, however, is every ten to fifteen years.

Silk-Oaks and Animals of the Fynbos

The symbol of the southern African flora is without doubt the silk-oak, which is the most common and characteristic flower of the fynbos. Its Latin family name, Proteaceae, was chosen by Linnaeus in 1735 to describe some of the native plants of Cape Province. The Swedish botanist Linnaeus was probably amazed by the great variety of species sharing a common flower and belonging to the same group. Perhaps for this reason he might have referred to the Greek God Proteus, who according to mythological tradition, was able to change appearance with great ease and to assume the most varied looks.

The silk-oak family makes up one of the oldest groups of angiosperms (flowering plants characterized by having seeds enclosed in an ovary, e.g., orchids and roses). It was already present in different forms in the ancient continent of Gondwana, more than 300 million years ago.

Presently, the silk-oak is widespread only in the Southern Hemisphere. Australia and South America share several species. All of southern Africa's silk-oaks are native, with only one species found also in Madagascar.

The silk-oaks vary greatly from shrubs to small trees. Its flowers, even the largest, are formed by many tubular elements gathered on the sepal (a leaflike member of the outer covering). On the edges of the sepal lies a crown of colorful bracts (leaves surrounding the flower) which make up a sort of petal. When this beautiful cover opens up, the real flower is still closed. A few days later, however, the flowers will suddenly bloom starting from the edges of the sepal. As soon as the corolla (outer envelope) of the flower reaches maturity, it separates into four parts that immediately wither, leaving the pistil (the seed-bearing organ of the flower) unprotected and pointing toward the sky. At this time the anthers (the sacs in the flower containing the pollen), which cover the internal surface of the corolla, deposit the pollen produced on the upper part of the pistil. The pistil looks enlarged because it has become a dispenser of pollen.

There are other types of silk-oaks which are characterized by small flower heads with incredibly long pistils. In fact, what makes these flowers so remarkable is not the corolla of spectacular bracts (in this case they are practi-

A cape sugarbird rests on a silk-oak. There are big differences between the male and the female of this species.

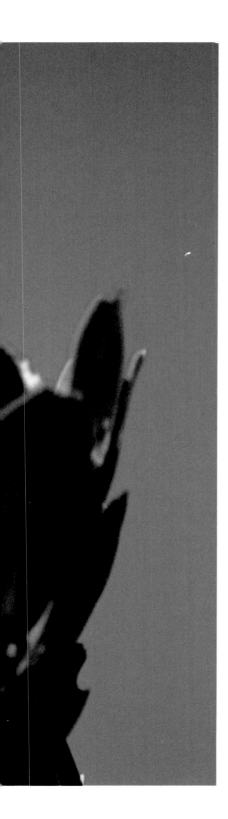

cally non-existent), but the bright colors of each individual flower and the mass of pistils with their enlarged tops. The pistils, as a whole, look like pins in a pin cushion.

The silk-oaks and heaths of the fynbos are the favorite habitats of sunbirds, which are small perching birds that feed on nectar. They fly quickly from flower to flower in search of nectar and small insects. These small and colorful birds, similar to the hummingbirds of America, have adapted by sucking nectar from flowers. They are able to stick their small tube-shaped beaks into the flower corollas, where they suck the nectar using their retractable tongues in the fashion of a straw. The split tongue is also useful for catching insects in flight, which are an important part of their diet.

The males and females of this species are very different from each other. The females have plumages of a plain color while the males display lively colors with metallic overtones. These sunbirds do not live only in the fynbos. They are present in virtually every type of environment from arid regions to humid forests, from high mountains to coastal dunes, anywhere insects are plentiful. Usually they land on flowers in order to feed. Rarely do they make the humming sound characteristic of hummingbirds in flight, even though they are able to hover for a certain amount of time by flapping their wings at high speeds.

The sunbirds fiercely defend their territory by displaying aggressive behavior, especially toward their own species. Among the various African species, the orange-breasted sunbird is the most common. Noisy and always active, it prefers mountain slopes where heath and silk-oaks abound, along the coast or at high elevations. It mates during the winter, that is, between May and August (in the Southern Hemisphere). The female lays one or two eggs and builds the nest among the branches of a small bush. The male, who does not take part in the brooding, helps in feeding the young.

The Cape sugarbird is also very common and it can be recognized by its long tail. Only two species of this bird are common to southern Africa and they are very similar to the Australian honeyeaters. In fact, they are so similar that until recently they were thought to belong to the same family.

Today, the striking resemblance among these two types of birds is considered more as a phenomenon of converging, or coming together of evolutionary forms rather than actual kinship.

It seems that the Cape sugarbirds originated independently in southern Africa. These small birds usually move from one elevation to another along the mountain slopes, according to the seasonal variations affecting the blossoming of the silk-oaks. They also feed on insects, especially during the mating season, when the females need to increase their protein intake. During this period, the males display themselves by flying with their long tail folded over their back and flapping their wings energetically. The mating season lasts from February to August (which are the winter months) when the silk-oaks are blossoming at the lower elevations.

Only the female builds the nest among the bushes, and it sits on the eggs until they hatch, after about seventeen days of incubation.

It is important to remember the role which these birds play in the environment. By continuously flying from one flower to another they act as the main pollen carriers for

heaths and silk-oaks. While searching for nectar in the colorful corollas, the fine pollen grains stick to the feathers of their heads. Thus, when the birds land on other flowers, they transfer the pollen onto the cavity of the pistil.

In addition to the birds, there are numerous insects which also transfer pollen. As strange as this may seem, even mice can transfer pollen. Many silk-oaks have flowers which come into contact with the ground. They are hidden among the vegetation and have duller colors. In this case, during the night, mice transfer the pollen from one flower to another with their snouts. In fact, mice are attracted to the silk-oaks by the nectar and by the sugary and meaty bracts of some species of these plants.

Even ants play an important role in the biological cycle of the silk-oaks. The seeds of some species have a whitish bulge rich in oily substances, of which ants are particularly fond. For this reason, seeds that have fallen to the ground are gathered by the ants and carried to their nests. Here, the oily substance of the seeds is eaten. The uneaten seeds are safely stored in the nest for many years until fire or other factors cause them to sprout.

Hummingbirds are conspicuous among the green environment of the fynbos. Their presence is continuously noticed because of their songs, their quick flying, and the fast flapping of their wings.

There are other more timid and elusive animals in this particular environment. The rhebok antelope, for example, prefers green valleys, hilly areas, or undisturbed flatlands near water. The male guides his family group, which consists of females and their young. The small duiker antelope measures only 22 inches (55 cm) at the shoulders. The male marks its territory by spraying the small branches with a secretion from its eye cavity glands.

This antelope is very territorial and refuses to move to a new territory even when it is preyed upon. Instead, it becomes nocturnal in order to remain in its original territory.

The Cape fox has a remarkable sense of hearing due to its large ears. Its sight is also very keen. The fox is always alert and ready to hide quickly among the vegetation. It is active at sunrise and during the night, but during the day it prefers to rest in its den.

Although the leopard is widespread, it is particularly adapted to the fynbos. It is not easy to observe this animal, although it is possible to identify its tracks in the wet soil.

The crocodile lives in groups along swamps, lakes and rivers where the vegetation is very thick. It is capable of ambushing large- and medium-size birds and mammals.

Since it is subject to extensive hunting, the leopard has been forced to become primarily nocturnal. This solitary animal enjoys lying in the sun and resting on trees and rocks. The leopard is both a superb climber and a good swimmer. It hunts small antelope, birds, snakes, fish, and domestic animals. Its favorite prey is the baboon, which is very common throughout the fynbos.

The Forest

In contrast with the rest of the African continent south of the Sahara, southern Africa does not have large areas covered by natural forests. In fact, forest areas are found only in the southern and eastern parts of southern Africa. Here, the abundant rainfall and hot climate result in a luxuriant vegetation. Favorable conditions for the forest are restricted to a narrow strip of land near the coast and to a few regions of the interior.

In addition to its limited geographical extension, the forest has also been damaged in the past. The destruction can be partially attributed to fires, but also to the extensive tree cutting brought about by logging activities.

Two types of forest can be distinguished. The first belongs to a cool and temperate climate, the second to a hot, subtropical climate. The temperate forest is unevenly distributed, with small strips located along the southern coast of Cape Province. Other strips of forest are located further inland, in isolated spots on the mountain slopes.

The largest section, which includes the well-known Tsitsikamma forest, consists of a strip of land approximately 112 miles (180 km) long and only 10 miles (16 km) wide. The undergrowth consists primarily of small bushes and ferns. Evergreen trees rise above this vegetation to a height of 33 to 66 feet (10 to 20 m). A large number of liana vines grow on these evergreens.

The yellowwood is an exceptional tree which grows to a height of 98 to 148 feet (30 to 45 m) and sometimes even reaches heights of 200 feet (60 m). This tree dominates the lower vegetation, and is in great demand as a source of lumber. Other tree species such as the stinkwood and the assegai are also well-known for their valuable wood.

The subtropical forest is limited to a strip of land along the eastern coast beginning at Port Elizabeth and ending toward the northeast. The effects of the warm ocean current and the abundant rainfall promote the growth of a luxuriant and thick vegetation.

This forest barely reaches inland from the coastal dunes, except along rivers. In this case, the forest, finding a favorable humid environment, follows the river course toward the interior.

Heading north, the variety of animals and plants increases. The vegetation becomes thicker and the whole forest acquires a more tropical appearance.

The trees, which are mostly evergreens, reach heights that vary between 16 and 33 feet (5 and 10 m). These trees are therefore lower than those found in the temperate forest.

Forest life, unlike other ecosystems that are spread out on a horizontal plane, is distributed in vertical layers. The density of trees is such that branches come in contact with one another. Branches intertwine and lie upon one another forming a continuous green cover. Between the highest and lowest points, a series of medium-size trees provide other layers. Each layer harbors numerous mini-environments and provides food and shelter for a great variety of animals.

Birds of the Forest

Several birds have adapted themselves quite well to forest life. These animals have evolved a quite efficient communication system due perhaps to the poor visibility caused by the dense vegetation. They emit loud, ear-piercing calls that enable them to communicate and defend their territories. Many birds also have a strong tendency to gather in large groups. Flocks of different insect-eating species are frequently seen feeding together.

According to some scientists, it is easier for these birds to find insects by working together as a group. This situation arises because the birds that feed among the vegetation of the underbrush scare off insects, which in turn fly upward where they are caught by other birds living in the upper layers of vegetation. The "upper" birds, in turn, cause the

Opposite page: The dense forest of the coastal park of Tsitsikamma. Giant trees, such as the yellowwood, prevail here. The undergrowth has many ferns, wild orchids, and a great variety of lilies.

The republican sparrow, common in dry areas, builds its giant nest among the strong branches of large trees. This bird stays rather close to its nest. It leaves for brief periods, returning with food and twigs for its nest.

insects in the trees to fall to the ground, where they are preyed upon by the ground feeders.

The crowned eagle is a magnificent bird of prey with camouflaged feathers that are well-suited for the type of environment in which it lives. The short but wide wings allow quick maneuvering and vertical takeoffs among thick vegetation. Its powerful feet enable the eagle to capture monkeys, hyraxes, and even larger animals, such as the duiker antelope.

The eagle does not hunt by hovering high in the sky, but prefers ambushing its prey. While waiting for its prey, the eagle perches quietly on a branch, among the dense foliage. Then it lunges at its victim. If the eagle is not able to surprise its prey, it silently follows the target by jumping from branch to branch until the right opportunity presents itself. This species is now threatened by extinction. In certain areas, the eagle is likely to disappear due to the destruction of its habitat brought about by fires or by the direct or indirect action of humans.

Other animal species are found in the dense vegetation where the environment is wet and swampy. The elegant dwarf rail (a marsh bird with characteristic brown plumage and short wings adapted for short flights) is rather difficult to observe, even though it is quite common. Its peculiar call, which only the males can make, has a mournful and ghostly quality. The natives attribute this sound to other animals such as snakes, chameleons, lizards, vipers, etc., but never to a bird.

The touraco inhabits both the savanna and the dense forests. This bird is known for the bright color of its feathers and for its ability to run quickly among tree branches.

The Delegorgue dove is a very rare tree bird that prefers the highest layers of the forest. Its habits are not well-known. It can be seen flying singly or in pairs, and its presence is revealed by an unmistakable call, a series of "coo, coo . . ." sounds.

There is another dove (timpanistria dove) which can be found only in the subtropical forest. It feeds on various seeds and on termites. The agility of this bird is amazing, especially its ability to fly between branches without colliding with the thick vegetation.

The Cape parrot is the largest parrot in southern Africa. It is rather common, yet limited to the habitat of the temperate forest. Usually it can be seen in small groups climbing trees or flying while shrieking loudly. Groups of these noisy parrots always make noise while they search for food.

The river hog has found an ideal habitat in the forest. The color of its coat varies from reddish brown to black. Long, pointed ears with a tuft of hair protrude from its head.

The turaco, a distant relative of the cuckoo, must not be overlooked. This bird displays the most beautiful feathers, a long tail and a crest. Certain species inhabit the savanna. Their feathers have a unique red color that is produced by a substance that contains copper. This type of pigment is very rare in the animal world. The green color is caused by the presence of green pigments and not by light refraction (the deflection of a light ray from a straight path), as is the case in most birds. The turacos eat fruit and live in the highest layers of the forest.

Another beautiful species is the emerald cuckoo. The plumage of this bird has a bright metallic-green color in the upper parts, with a lemon-yellow color around the abdomen. The emerald cuckoo inhabits the highest limbs of the largest trees, where it feeds on fruits and caterpillars. Although it is hard to spot, it is easily identifiable by its call, which sounds like a whispered "Hello Audrey."

The narina trogon is rightly considered the most elegant bird in southern Africa. It flies very quietly and behaves like a giant flycatcher. This bird perches motionless on a branch for long periods of time and occasionally flies away in pursuit of an insect.

The barbets are among the best-known groups of small birds. These birds are related to the woodpeckers, and like their relatives, display lively colors with many shades ranging from yellow to green, brown, white, and black. They spend much of their time feeding among the highest branches of trees. The barbets build nests by drilling with their beaks into the trunks of dead trees.

This group includes a few rare species, for example the green barbet, which is one of the rarest localized birds in all of southern Africa. The only known population lives in the Ngoye forest, south of the Zambezi River.

The Cape broadbill, with its large beak and short tail, is similar to a flycatcher in size and appearance. This bird is the only southern African representative of the broadbill family, although several species inhabit the forests of Asia.

The list of southern African birds has certainly not been completely covered. It continues with the fruit-eating bulbul, woodpeckers busy drilling the bark of trees in search of insects, and the shy thrushes rummaging among the dead leaves on the ground.

The Woodward flycatcher only inhabits subtropical environments. It lives within an area where the vegetation and underbrush are very thick. This bird can often be spot-

The hippopotamus lives in herds consisting of up to several dozen animals. It lives mainly in or near lakes, rivers, or large swamps.

ted on the ground in small groups or in pairs.

The forests are also inhabited by the sunbirds. One of the most beautiful species is the collared sunbird. The feathers of this bird are of a bright metallic-green color, while its abdomen is covered with canary-yellow-colored feathers. The sunbird prefers the underbrush where it feeds on small insects and fruits. Its nest has a peculiar pear-shape and hangs from branches at a height of 13 to 16 feet (4 to 5 m) from the ground.

Other Animals

The forest animals include various mammals which can easily be overlooked by an inattentive observer. Obviously, one must have plenty of patience to silently search through the leaves and shrubs. It should be kept in mind that these animals are able to perfectly camouflage themselves. Furthermore, many of these mammals are most active at dawn and at dusk.

The large African waterhog can be spotted during the day, but only in areas where it is not harassed by hunters. It hides among dense, low vegetation and feeds on bulbs, roots, fruits, seeds, small animals, and birds. This wild pig lives in family groups, sometimes numbering twenty ani-

mals, led by an adult male.

More rarely one may encounter old solitary males. The females, which give birth twice a year, build a grassy bedding where the young remain for a few days. This species is unique in being the only mammal common to both Africa and Madagascar.

The forest also provides a shelter for larger animals. The buffalo, for example, which seems to move like a shadow among the trees, is active in the early morning and in the evening. During the day the buffalo enjoys resting along riverbanks or pools of water.

The nyala lives in forests and areas near water. It is active mainly in the early morning or late afternoon. In areas where it feels threatened, this antelope had developed nocturnal habits.

The waterways are also inhabited by hippopotamuses and crocodiles. Crocodiles are among the most fearful water predators of the forest. They are able to attack even small buffalo and antelope.

The leopard, which thrives in any type of environment, is one of the most able hunters of the forest. However, when necessary, the leopard settles for small vertebrates (animals with a backbone). These prey are dragged up into the foliage of trees, where the leopard quietly devours them.

The tree mammals are extremely numerous, with many species of squirrels, bats, and monkeys. These animals feed primarily on fruits and leaves. At night one can hear an amazingly loud call, which mixes in with the calls of birds of prey and insects. This loud noise is made by the hyraxes, which announce their territories from high in the treetops.

The underbrush provides shelter for the small duiker antelopes, which are well-adapted to the forest environment. The most common in these areas is the Natal duiker, which is 20 inches (50 cm) tall, and weighs a little over 20 lbs (10 kg). The bodies of this type of antelope are well-suited to the requirements of the environment. Aside from being small in size, the body of the duiker has an arched back and a roundish shape. Its legs are small and thin, the front legs being shorter than the rear legs, while its small horns are straight, without branches, and slightly inclined toward the back. This shape prevents the animal from becoming entangled among branches and bushes. The diet of the duiker antelope is based on grasses and fruits.

They may travel alone or in pairs during the mating season. At this time, the male runs in front of the female and rubs its scent glands (located in front of its eyes) against her snout. It is very likely that the duiker antelope has adapted to the forest environment after having evolved from species which originated in open areas such as the steppes and savannas.

The bushbuck antelope has a similar body shape. Its horns are spiral-shaped and spread apart. The coat displays a series of stripes and spots arranged in such a way as to offer excellent camouflage. Males and females live in different, though sometimes overlapping territories.These animals mark their territories by rubbing the soil with the secretions of their scented glands. The bushbuck antelope feeds on leaves, grasses, fruits, and buds.

The small suni antelope is found only in a few areas and is no taller than 16 inches (40 cm). This animal is presently considered a rare and endangered species.

MADAGASCAR

"Here in Madagascar, Mother Nature seems to have withdrawn into a private sanctuary in order to develop life forms that are different from those found elsewhere. At each step, one encounters the most unusual and amazing plants and animals." This is how the French botanist Philibert Commerson described this large island in 1771. He also defined Madagascar as the "naturalist's heaven." Indeed, Commerson had good reasons for stating this.

Geology and Topography

After Greenland, Borneo, and New Guinea, Madagascar is the fourth largest island in the world. Because of its natural characteristics, this land can be considered as a true miniature continent. A long and deep sea channel separates Madagascar from Africa. This is known as the Mozambique Channel, whose width varies from 218 to 750 miles (350 to 1,200 km). As for its geographic position, Madagascar is located almost completely in a tropical weather area and it is surrounded by the southern Indian Ocean. The island is located between the 11° 57' east and 25° 32' latitude south. Its length runs parallel to the adjoining African coast. The island, which is about 1,000 miles (1,600 km) long, covers a surface of 227,800 square miles (590,000 sq. km.)

Once part of the ancient continent of Gondwana, Madagascar is certainly of a continental origin. Its geologic structure is made up of highly metamorphic pre-Cambrian rocks (over 600 million years old), which in certain places crop up to the surface. For the most part, however, the surface is covered by clay belonging to the Tertiary period (from 65 to 5 million years ago).

Along the center of the island there is a group of mountain peaks. These mountains form a plateau with an average elevation of 4,900 feet (1,500 m). In a section that has been highly carved by erosion and volcanic activity, the plateau reaches an elevation of 8,500 feet (2,600 m). Certain peaks of volcanic origin, such as Maromokotra in the central massif of the Tsaratanana, reach 9,500 feet (2,887 m). The plateau falls abruptly along its eastern edge with an impressive rough slope which continues further down along the coast. On the western edge, the central massif descends more gradually in relation to the sedimentary basins of the Morondava and the Majunga. Another sedimentary expanse can be encountered further north, beyond the Ampasindava peninsula.

The original wedge of Madagascar's western side dates

Opposite page: The special reserve of Nosy Mangab is located on a small island in the Bay of Antongil. It is famous for its rain forest, the last habitat of the rare aye-aye lemur.

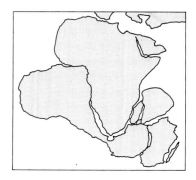

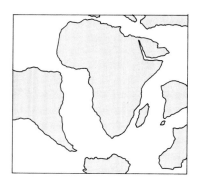

Above: Madagascar was once part of the ancient continent of Gondwana. Starting from the Jurassic period, Madagascar began to drift away. The total isolation of this island-continent that followed explains in part the peculiarity of Madagascan plants and animals.

Opposite page: The map of the different domains according to the researcher Humbert *(above);* July and January temperatures *(center);* rainfall map of Madagascar *(bottom).*

back to the continental drift. Geologists have not been able to identify with certainty the exact period of its formation. Some believe that Madagascar was once located along the northeast African coast between present day Somalia and Tanzania. Other geologists hold that Madagascar was once located next to Mozambique and that it later drifted toward the east. Still others believe it was located along the Natal coast and later drifted north and east. A final hypothesis suggests that Madagascar was once located in the same area which it presently occupies, and it was later separated by the African continent by the formation of the Mozambique Channel.

At any rate, it seems that the separation and the drift occurred during the middle of the Jurassic period (a period of the Mesozoic era). At this time Africa and Madagascar were separated by the Mozambique Channel. Consequently, Madagascar remained attached to India's southwest coast until the Paleocene period, when the two continents finally separated.

Climate

Taking into consideration the extension and the uneven topography of Madagascar, it is easy to understand how its climate is extremely varied. Generally speaking there are two main seasons: summer (November through April) and winter (May through October). These seasons are joined together by transitional periods. Nevertheless, certain seasonal variations are of local character as they are tied to topographical factors. By crossing the island from north to south, at sea level one notices that the average median temperature decreases substantially. For example, from the 80°F (27°C) of Diego Suarez, we go down to 73°F (23°C) in Fort Dauphin.

Even inland the same decrease in temperature prevails, though complicated by the altitude, since the temperature also decreases as the altitude does. On the western coast the temperature is slightly higher than the temperature registered on the east coast at the same latitude. The highest temperatures occur in January and February in most of the east coast, in November in the plateau, and in January through March in the southwestern area.

It is possible to subdivide Madagascar according to bio-climatic areas by taking into consideration temperature, rainfall, and seasonal factors. Consequently, the plateau—above 2,300 feet (700 m)—is considered as having a

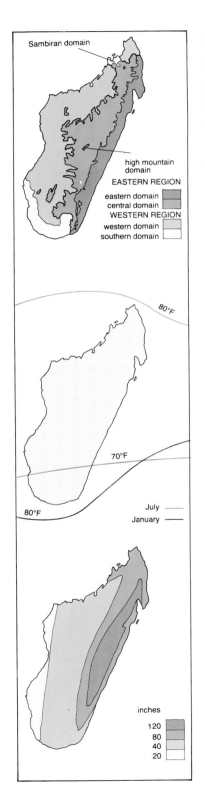

Sambiran domain

high mountain
domain
EASTERN REGION
eastern domain
central domain
WESTERN REGION
western domain
southern domain

80°F

70°F

80°F

July
January

inches
120
80
40
20

temperate climate with easily identifiable wet and dry seasons. The eastern slopes, though humid, vary in temperature according to altitude. The area at the extreme south of the island and Cape d'Ambre in the north are hot and semi-arid with irregular rainfall and possible periods of drought.

The low western lands are hot and subject to rainfall with seasonal peaks. However, further south, these same areas have a drier climate. Finally, the Sambiran region, located north of the western lands, is known for a hotter and more humid climate, similar to the climate of the East.

Vegetation

To a great extent, the present vegetation of Madagascar represents only a trace of what it must have been before the arrival of people. Asian sailors occupied the island about two thousand years ago. Centuries of destruction of the original forest, agriculturization of extensive areas, and forest fires accompanied by soil erosion, led to the almost total disappearance of original vegetation. Often these destructive elements brought permanent damage to the entire unique ecosystems.

The damage can be clearly seen while flying by airplane over central Madagascar. Wide expanses of red soil can be spotted with fragments of vegetation at its edges. Despite this generally bleak outlook, however, a few plant and animal communities have survived to this day, though only in limited areas. In any case, both plant and animal life are always in danger of extinction. Their survival is strictly linked to the future decisions of the inhabitants of Madagascar. Although many environments in Madagascar have been modified, a large number of native plant species can be found on this island. (The same situation exists for the animals, as we shall later see.) Eighty percent of the plant species found in Madagascar are native. In certain districts as much as 50 percent of the flora is native at the genre, or type level. The great differences in climate, the countless geological structures of the island, and evolution itself have had an extraordinary effect on the distribution, variety, and abundance of plant life in Madagascar.

The Western Region

The hot western region is characterized by the western and southern domains. Different types of soil determine several of the main features of the forest associated with the western domain. Deciduous woodlands of tamarind trees

Above: A few typical plants of Madagascar are seen. Starting at the top, the tamarind tree, which bears large pods full of a refreshing pulp. The baobab, present in Madagascar with seven native species, is famous for its swollen trunks and stumpy branches. The flower of the flamboyant tree, a native species, has been introduced in many tropical countries because of its spectacular flowers.

Opposite page: Two native Madagascan plants in the small botanical garden of the Berenty Natural Reserve near Fort Dauphin. One is a didierea with a spiny and fleshy trunk. The other in full bloom, is a *Delonix regia.*

are prevalent here. These yellow-flowered trees generally grow along river valleys where the soil is moist and rich with silica minerals. The trees form a continuous green canopy with heights of 26 to 50 feet (8 to 15 m). Scattered here and there are some trees as high as 65 feet (20 m). The underbrush is quite thin. In the areas with limestone soil the landscape changes and the forest is replaced by a vegetation of drought-tolerant plants (xerophytes). These are plants that grow in dry, hot climates, like the cactus.

A grassy type of savanna often replaces the original forest. This savanna is subject to periodic fires. The few surviving forest trees stand out over the wide expanse. Here there are succulent plants such as bryophyllums and aloes, resinous plants such as the myrrh tree, and the peculiarly-shaped spurges, with flattened branches.

The baobab tree has a gigantic, swelled profile which is silhouetted against the sky. An umbrella of short, thick, and barren branches opens at the top of its strange trunk. It is commonly thought that the baobab is only found in Africa. Actually, Africa has only one species of baobab, while Madagascar has seven species, all of which are different from each other and distributed throughout the island.

These trees are useful to the natives. The oil from the seeds, which are contained in long pods, is edible. Furthermore, the trunk has fiber soaked with water which can be fed to domestic livestock during droughts, when other types of food are scarce, or when the pastures are not yet ready. In addition, the trunk of the baobab can be carved into boats or water containers.

The southern semi-arid area is considered one of the most amazing environments within Madagascar. It is characterized by a bush type of vegetation which varies slightly according to the height reached by the drought-tolerant plants and by the types of plant communities present in the area. The adaptation of single plant species to this hostile environment is very well-known. The struggle to avoid excessive water loss has led to the parallel development of similar plant structures in certain plants belonging to entirely different families. Their enlarged roots hold more water.

Other plants have transformed their leaves into thorns or have reduced the size of their leaves considerably in order to reduce water losses from transpiration (the giving off of water vapor from leaf pores).

Species of bryophyllums have leaves and stems covered

by waxy secretions or thick, hairlike structures. These devices reduce evaporation to a minimum. The Jatropha spurge sheds all of its leaves during the dry season. It survives this unfavorable period in a sort of "dormant" state.

An overview of the southern bush is not complete without a description of the didierea plants, otherwise called "octopus trees." These peculiar trees, which are common in southwestern Madagascar, are succulents and therefore well-suited to dry environments. Their enlarged, cylinder-shaped branches spread out in all directions from a short cylindric trunk, as if they were huge tentacles. The surface of the green branches and of the trunk is covered by clusters of small leaves and sharp spines arranged at regular intervals. These leaves and spines vary in number and shape according to the type of plant.

Some of the didiereas can reach a height of 33 to 50 feet (10 to 15 m) with long branches pointing upward toward the sky. Other species at first grow horizontal branches along the ground before sprouting branches from the center that point skyward. These vertical branches will then give rise to a tuft of horizontal branches.

The pulpy branches of certain species produce small bunches of flowers at their tips.

The family of spurges is also widespread in this area. These plants have adapted themselves quite well to this harsh environment. A well-known group of these plants is treelike in appearance and has modified green or grayish branches. For this reason it has been named the coral-shaped spurge.

The spurge *Euphorbia oncoclada* is a larger shrub with a spherical shape. Its branches do not have leaves or thorns. They are cylindrical segments of a silver-green color with a narrowing where the secondary branches start, and where the buds are also located. Therefore, the entire plant appears somewhat like a "sausage." Another common species of spurge has flat branches and an umbrella shape. It can reach 16 feet (5 m) in height, making it the tallest spurge in Madagascar.

One of the dogbane plants (having milky juice and bell-shaped flowers) present in the bush is the strange "elephant legs." It is a tree with a single, vertical trunk similar to a swelled column, completely covered by small groups of spines. At the top of the trunk there are a few branches ending with clusters of long leaves. During the blossoming season these branches are covered by showy white and

The dogbane plants of the *Pachypodium* genus include various native forms having succulent, bottle-shaped trunks with sharp thorns and clusters of leaves at their top.

Opposite page: There are about sixty species of bryophyllums *(top)* in Madagascar. Like the stonecrops *(bottom)*, these are succulent plants that thrive on rocky soils. The aloe *(center)*, of which about fifty Madagascan species are known, grows mostly in arid and rocky environments. They prefer particular types of soil.

yellow flowers. The trunk of this tree holds a large amount of liquid.

Certain species of small baobab trees are also found in the bush. They can be easily recognized because of their bottle-shaped trunks. One type of baobab, characterized by small, pointed leaves and yellow flowers, can only be found in the basin of the Mandrare River. This plant can often be found together with certain didiereas and it can reach a height of 65 feet (20 m).

The native traveler's palm is a longtime symbol of Madagascar because of its elegant fan of unfolded leaves. It can be found in large clusters on the eastern hills up to an elevation of about 2,000 feet (610 m). A considerable amount of water is stored at the base of its leaves. This water, however, is infested with insect larvae and microorganisms and is not safe to drink.

The Eastern Region

The eastern region is generally more humid. Since the plant species of this region differ more among themselves, this area displays a greater variety of plants. The eastern region is well-known for its dense, luxuriant rain forests which reach an altitude of 2,600 feet (800 m), while the evergreen forest of this region consists of trees that can reach a height of up to 199 feet (30 m). An enormous number of different plant species are widespread and separated from each other according to altitude.

The lower layer of the forest is of a relatively open type. Liana vines and epiphytes such as orchids and ferns abound

on trunks and branches. Tree trunks, branches, and leaf edges are covered by lichen plants. (A lichen is composed of a fungus and algae.)

Numerous species of palms also grow in these forests. The palm tree family has the highest number of native species in Madagascar. Madagascar also has about thirty species of screw pine trees. Typical among these is the traveler's tree, a palm with enormous fan-shaped leaves.

Climbing to an altitude between 2,625 and 4,265 feet (800 to 1,300 m) one reaches the eastern part of the central domain.

The medium elevation rain forest is still luxuriant, but it has fewer layers than the same forest at lower altitudes. The height reached by the trees is almost the same and their foliage forms a continuous canopy of leaves at about 100 feet (30 m). An underbrush of grasses and bushes grows at the base of these trees. Several types of epiphytic plants grow here, including orchids.

At higher altitudes—up to 6,600 feet (2,000 m)—a lichen forest of tree-shaped plants with hard and thick leaves predominates. Their trunks can reach a height of up to 40 feet (12 m) and their branches are literally covered with epiphytic plants. In the lichen forest there are also native orchids, stonecrops, ferns with delicate leaves, and bushes of mountain heath.

The high mountain domain is limited to the highest peaks of the country and it is characterized by a shrub vegetation. Rare native plant species grow on the rocks.

Descending toward the western slopes of the central domain, the climate becomes warmer and drier in relation to the climate of the eastern slopes. Here the landscape is dominated by forests of rather short trees having hard, thick leaves, along with a bushy undergrowth.

This brief description of the forests of Madagascar refers to the original native species of plants. It should be kept in mind, however, that a substantial portion of Madagascar's vegetation is no longer the original primitive vegetation. In fact, a large part of the central plateau has now been deforested. Wide expanses of what was once a forest have been converted to agriculture, particularly rice paddies. At the same time, eucalyptus trees have been introduced almost throughout the island. The lowlands in the west have been transformed into prairies and the wet forests of the east have been largely replaced by the savoka (a secondary type of forest with dense, rapid-growing vegetation).

THE MAMMALS

According to paleontologists (those who study fossils), mammals began to establish themselves in Madagascar in successive waves which started in the Paleocene period and ended in the Pliocene period. As far as "recent" mammals are concerned, Madagascar has only six different large groups. Yet, within these few groups there are many native species. Much later, with the arrival of humans about two thousand years ago, mammals from other continents were introduced, either intentionally or by chance. For example, the oxen, horses, sheep, pigs, cats, dogs, and the Asian civet cat were brought to this island by people.

Other undesirable animals such as mice, rats, and shrews were also introduced by people. Nevertheless, the first real "settlers" of Madagascar were certain insect-eaters from the Paleocene period.

During the Paleocene period, the Mozambique Channel was probably much narrower than its present size. For this reason, certain primitive insect-eating mammals were able to cross the channel by chance, clinging to floating branches and logs drifting with the current to Madagascar. From these animals there later evolved the native tenrec family, which includes small, insect-eating mammals of Madagascar.

Certain species of primitive lemurs, the ancestors of today's lemurs, also arrived in Madagascar by chance using the same means.

In the Pleistocene period, a native species of hippopotamus of African origin found its way to Madagascar through unknown circumstances. Unfortunately this animal is now extinct. Another hoofed animal is the African river hog, which is quite common on the island. It was probably introduced by people in prehistoric times from nearby Africa.

The Tenrec Family

The family of the tenrecs is native to Madagascar and it includes at least thirty species. These animals have evolved in various stages of adaptation, originating from a common ancestor. Generally, these insect-eaters have rather squat bodies and a size that varies between a large rabbit and a mouse. Their snouts end with a small nose. These animals also have rather primitive body structures. The eyes and tail are smaller in certain species, while other species have spiny coats that are an effective defense against predators.

From a common genetic model, the tenrecs adapted in

Opposite page: The sifaka lemurs include several local species with different body colors. All these species display complex group behavior. Group behavior is based on a small family core: usually two parents and two or three young animals of various ages. When environmental conditions become harsh, families often merge into one group consisting of a dozen animals. Until the age of one month, the tiny lemur hangs to the mother's abdominal hair. Later it is carried on its back. Only at the age of three to four months will it be able to move on its own among the branches and to play with other group members.

The large nocturnal tenrec is common in Madagascar. It lives inside dens burrowed in the soil. It can weigh up to 7 pounds (3 kg). For this reason, the tenrec has been introduced also in the Seychelles Islands and at Réunion, where the natives value its meat.

different ways during the course of evolution. Isolation was an influential factor in this development. Some tenrecs are tree-dwellers; another type is similar to the mole in the way it digs underground tunnels. Another has a spiny coat and lives in the underbrush. At the approach of danger it curls into a ball like the porcupine. Still others have a tail that is flattened vertically, small eyes, and webbed feet. These features reflect their aquatic habits.

The reproductive characteristics of the tenrecs vary according to different species. The long-tailed tenrec gives birth to only two young at one time. The common tenrec, however, can give birth to about thirty young. In this last case, however, only half of the young will survive because the female cannot feed all thirty.

The ground tenrecs are interesting because of their behavior. They are able to locate prey in the dark (earthworms, small vertebrates, and insects) by using an echo system. Many of these animals are active at night or at dusk.

In addition to a well-developed sense of hearing they have a keen sense of smell and a well-developed, efficient sense of touch. During the winter they often fall into a state of sleep which is similar to hibernation. At this time they take shelter in holes or underground dens or inside tree stumps. The tenrecs hibernate only after having stored fat in their tissues to supply the energy needed for their metabolism during hibernation. In its native territory the tenrec inhabits hot and sandy areas with low shrubs. The small striped tenrec is quite common. These animals are about 8 inches (20 cm) long and have bright colors—three white and yellow stripes running lengthwise, which contrast with a black back. The tenrec has a bristly coat, and the top of its very pointed snout has a cluster of spines. Its back has eleven to eighteen spines that are thick at the base. These spines are a defense and also give a warning when the animal is threatened. The tenrec is fond of snails and worms. It is nocturnal and burrows a maze of tunnels in the ground.

The hedgehog tenrec lives in bushy areas and in semiarid regions. It is an omnivorous animal (feeding on both animals and plants) and, when threatened, curls into a ball. A series of sharp, grayish white quills are deeply embedded in its coat and constitute a protection against the attacks of predators.

The rice tenrec should be mentioned separately. This animal is quite common in the northeast and on the pla-

teaus. Little, however, is known of its biological characteristics. Because it feeds on insects and other ground invertebrates, the rice tenrec digs tunnels where the soil is moist. By doing so it uproots small rice plants and damages the embankments of rice paddies, causing severe problems to local farmers.

In some ways, the rice tenrec is like the North American mole. Likewise, the water tenrec is quite similar to the water-shrew of the temperate areas. It lives along riverbanks, creeks, and swamps. Because of its webbed hind feet and its long, flat, oar-like tail, the water tenrec is an excellent swimmer and diver. In the water it hunts for small frogs, insects, and shellfish.

Civets and Mongooses

Unlike the insect-eaters and the lemurs, the civet and mongooses did not evolve into diversified species with different adaptations once they colonized Madagascar. It is probable that all of the Madagascar civets and mongooses have a common origin.

The large Madagascar hedgehog is a native insect-eating tenrec that resembles the porcupine due to its thick, quill-like dorsal spines.

The fanaloka is a native civet that prefers moist environments. It preys mostly on aquatic animals. This small carnivore is so dependent on water that some sources believe it cannot survive for even twenty-four hours without drinking.

Generally monogamous (having one mate), they live in a forest habitat and give birth to one young. About 31 inches (80 cm) long, the fanaloka civet is active at night or dusk. These animals live strictly on the ground and have long snouts and a cylindrical tail. The fanaloka civet can be recognized at first glance by its light brown coat with spots and stripes and a ringed tail. It hunts on the ground level for rodents, frogs, and invertebrates. It does not hibernate during the unfavorable season (June to August). Although food may become scarce, the fanaloka civet relies on abundant fat reserves stored under its entire skin.

The falanouc mongoose prefers the dense undergrowth of the wet forests in eastern and central Madagascar. Its diet is very particular. The falanouc feeds on shellfish, amphibians (frogs), insects, and a large amount of worms. Its small teeth and inability to climb trees are severe handicaps. The falanouc is often hunted by the natives for its meat. The numbers of this animal are steadily decreasing due to its inability to escape the natives and their dogs.

There are four species of related mongooses that inhabit Madagascar. These are the ring-tailed mongoose of the eastern evergreen forests, the narrow-striped mongoose of the deciduous woodlands of the west and southwest, the brown-tailed mongoose of the east coast, and the little-known, broad-striped mongoose of the wet forests of the eastern and central regions.

Generally speaking, they resemble weasels and minks and are less than 20 inches (50 cm) long with an 8-inch (20-cm) tail. Except for the broad-striped mongoose, all are active during the day and are excellent climbers. Their favorite prey are small, tree-living vertebrates and insects found among tree branches. The ring-tailed mongooses do not hesitate to enter the water in search of fish and small amphibians.

The diet of the narrow-striped mongoose varies somewhat according to the season. Generally, it feeds on small rodents and lemurs. However, when its favorite prey is not available, it also feeds on insects and their larvae.

According to a local legend, the narrow-striped mongoose, which is also fond of honey, protects itself from bee stings by covering its body with spider webs during its attacks on beehives.

The fossa cat is an excellent predator, and it is the largest carnivore of Madagascar. It is 5 feet (1.5 m) long and weighs up to 26 pounds (12 kg). Of all the mongooses and civets, it has most successfully taken advantage of the predator's niche in the ecosystem of Madagascar. It is quite common in the forests and also in the savannas.

In a few areas of the plateau it has been entirely killed off by humans. Active at dusk or at night, this mammal is a loner that needs a large territory for hunting purposes. It sleeps and finds shelter on trees, in holes, or in ant mounds. It marks the ground and trees of its territory with the scent secreted by its anal and genital glands. Its powerful teeth, retractable claws, and its long whiskers make it similar to a reddish puma-like cat with round ears and a long snout.

Three mongooses and one civet. *From top to bottom:* the ring-tailed mongoose, the broad-striped mongoose, the fossa cat and the falanouk mongoose. Madagascar hosts seven native species of mongooses and civets. In addition to these animals, there are three carnivores that were imported by humans: the jaboady, introduced by the first Indonesian navigators, and dogs and cats. These animals are frequently in the wild state and constitute a serious threat to the balance of the island's ecosystem.

Other Mammals

The rodents of Madagascar are very significant from an ecological and evolutionary standpoint. Together with the insect-eaters they form an important source of food for various types of predators. Aside from a few types of rats and mice introduced by humans, the only rodents present in Madagascar are in the Nesomys genus. It is possible that they descended from a primitive group of New World rodents. They have evolved in Madagascar into the present seventeen native species. These species, quite different from each other, have occupied many habitats in the forest.

The giant jumping rat of western Madagascar can be found in an area of only a few hundred square miles within the land owned by the De Heaulmes, a French family. Luckily, the De Heaulme family is very concerned with the protection of the environment. Their property will soon be handed over to a national foundation of Madagascar belonging to the World Wildlife Federation. The foundation will be responsible for the protection of this local animal.

Sucker-footed bats are native to the island of Madagascar. They are distant relatives of certain South American and New Zealand species.

The flying foxes (large bats) are better known since they are highly valued by the natives. Madagascar and the Pemba Island (near Zanzibar) represent the western limit of the geographical distribution of these Asian bats, which are altogether absent on the African mainland.

The flying foxes live in large colonies and can sometimes be seen flying in daylight. However, it is more common to see them at rest during the day, hanging upside down from the branches of large trees which rise above the canopy of the forest. They look like unusual hanging black fruits. The long wings composed of membranes cover the body. They have a typical fox snout with lively eyes. Their noises are reminiscent of a noisy chicken pen. The flying foxes fly to nearby agricultural areas or to fruit-filled trees of the forest.

Lemurs

Madagascar is well-known for its lemurs (arboreal primates). According to the latest research the apes and monkeys owe their evolutionary development to the lemurs. This evolutionary development is not easy to trace from the fossils which have been found to date. In fact, researchers have come across "empty" spaces in the evolu-

The flying foxes of Madagascar are fruit-eaters that feed on bananas, dates, mangoes, flowers and various fruits. They often cause serious damage to plantations. One should not forget, however, the important role played by these bats in support of the ecosystem. They carry and spread pollen in large areas among various types of vegetation.

tionary process which makes the interpretation of the Madagascar species all the more difficult. The first lemurs were present in Europe, North America, and Africa since the Paleocene period.

A group of these lemurs could have invaded Madagascar during the Eocene period by crossing the Mozambique Channel through floating vegetation.

According to another theory, a chain of islands existed between Africa and Madagascar. The lemurs could have gradually made their way across these islands, eventually reaching Madagascar. The island bridges would have later disappeared, following the movements of the earth's crust, isolating these primitive lemurs from the rest of the world.

The ring-tailed lemurs gather in groups that display a well-organized ranking structure. Their territories are particularly stable. Within these territories the groups walk from one place to another, sometimes covering distances of over one-half mile (1 km). The females dominate within the group and are responsible for defending the group from nearby rivals. The defense is carried out by vocal exchanges. The ring-tailed lemur is able to produce a great variety of sounds. At times the warning cry of a single member evokes a chorus of sounds from the entire group. Barking sounds are directed to predators. Sharp, piercing sounds warn the lemur of approaching birds of prey, several of which prey on young lemurs.

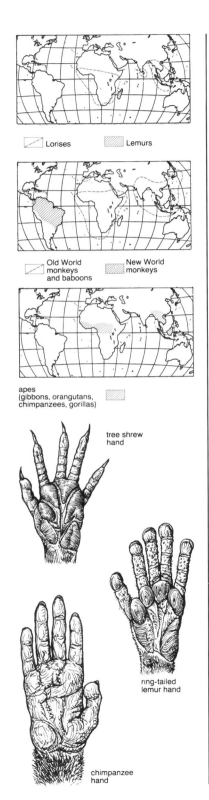

Lorises   Lemurs

Old World monkeys and baboons   New World monkeys

apes (gibbons, orangutans, chimpanzees, gorillas)

tree shrew hand

ring-tailed lemur hand

chimpanzee hand

Later, during the Oligocene period (about thirty million years ago) monkeys evolved from animals that had never crossed the Mozambique Channel. These monkeys spread through Africa, where they occupied the available environments. The rare groups of lemurs which remained on the African continent were thus restricted to only a few areas. These primitive lemurs developed into the pottos and the galagos, which are forerunners of the African monkeys. These lemurs are solitary insect-eaters that are active at night.

The primitive lemurs that migrated to Madagascar had practically no competitors. In this "mini-continent," lacking large predators, the lemurs found luxuriant forests and a variation of climatic conditions. Here they had the opportunity to occupy numerous ecological niches similar to those that were occupied by the African monkeys. The lack of herbivores also contributed to their quick reproduction. Thus the lemurs of Madagascar soon became part of a great evolutionary process. They were able to evolve into considerably different forms, colors, sizes, etc.

Like a large natural laboratory, the different geographical and environmental conditions of the island brought about, through time, new forms of adaptation and new features. These changes were passed down to the descendants of the original lemurs.

There are a few species of dwarf lemurs that are commonly found in forest trees throughout the island. Their large eyes betray their preference for night activity. They actively move about on trees and shrubs, where they may build nests made of leaves.

Sometimes they take shelter in the holes of rotting tree trunks. It is not hard to spot these animals in the forest at night, but the observer should wear a helmet with a light, such as those used by cave explorers. The eyes of the small lemurs shine in the dark when struck by the beam of light. It is indeed an amazing experience to suddenly discover how many of these creatures inhabit the forest and move about at night.

Mouse lemurs are the smallest of these animals. They are less than 10 inches (25 cm) long, and their tail accounts for about half their length. Mouse lemurs are common in the eastern, western, and Sambiran forests. Their origins are not well-known. They feed on fruits, flowers, insects, and sometimes on small rodents. They are able to capture and eat newly hatched birds with their small hands. The mouse

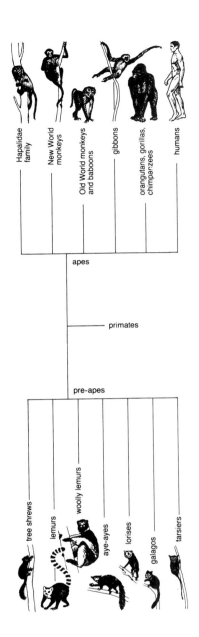

apes

primates

pre-apes

tree shrews

lemurs

woolly lemurs

aye-ayes

lorises

galagos

tarsiers

Hapalidae family

New World monkeys

Old World monkeys and baboons

gibbons

orangutans, gorillas, chimpanzees

humans

Top: The classic subdivision of pre-apes, primates, and apes with the most typical forms.

Opposite page, top: These three charts show the world distribution of pre-apes, New World monkeys, Old World monkeys, and apes.

Opposite page, bottom: The hand of a tree shrew is compared to those of the ring-tailed lemur and the chimpanzee.

lemurs are also fond of tree sap and of the sugary substances found on leaves and along tender stems. The plants secrete this substance after certain insects puncture the leaves.

The mouse lemurs can be easily spotted licking this sugary substance during the night. Both male and female take part in rearing the young. The noises they make include warning screams and communication sounds.

In the eastern, western, and southern forests larger types of lemurs can be found. The larger lemurs are lazier than the mouse lemurs in their movements among the trees. Like the smaller lemurs, they are fond of fruits, flowers, and nectar, as well as sap and pollen. They hunt insects and small vertebrate climbers such as the chameleon, which they swallow after having grabbed them with their hands. During the dry season, they hibernate and live on the fat stored under their skin.

Another representative of the same family, the fork-marked lemur, is also a fruit-eater who marks the branches and tree bark of its territory with a secretion from a gland located under the neck. The fork-marked lemur is a lively animal and a true nocturnal acrobat. It is capable of judging distances in the dark without making any mistakes. The fork-marked lemur is more common in the Mangoky and Sambiran forests and on D'Ambre Mountain.

The best-known lemurs are the gentle-lemurs and the lemurs of the Varecia genus. These animals are active during the day or at dusk. Their diet is mainly vegetarian. They are pretty animals with large eyes, pointed snouts, and long tails. Their coat displays various bright, contrasting colors, depending on the species and, in certain cases, the sex.

These lemurs run along branches and leap from one tree to the other with amazing agility, while keeping their body in a horizontal position. If they have to cover longer distances on the ground in search of food or drink, they will jump on all four legs.

Lemurs have highly developed group instincts. They live in groups of about twenty animals, usually led by females. Each female gives birth to one young, rarely to two or three at a time. For a certain period of time the newborn clings to the mother's fur or is carried on her back.

There are six species of common lemurs. These species have been classified by biologists according to numerous geographical types, the coloration of their coats, and their chromosomes.

Like other lemurs, the macaco lemur species is mainly vegetarian. These agile pre-apes can cover considerable distances in the forest in search of food. Leaves, flowers, and fruits are nibbled from branches. The lemur folds each small branch with its hands and then brings this food to its mouth after having smelled, analyzed, and carefully selected it.

The macaco lemur is approximately the size of a large cat with a long tail. It is restricted to the western part of Northern Madagascar and also to the islands of Nosy Be and Nosy Komba. The male and female of this species have a different physical appearance. The fur of the adult males is of a beautiful, shiny black color, while that of the females is of a golden reddish brown color. During the day, these lemurs move in groups among the trees. They almost never come into contact with the ground. At dawn they resume their wanderings.

The composition of the group follows a typical pattern. A few males and females are the leaders, while the younger animals follow the leaders closely.

Lemurs spend time grooming each other. They also mark branches and bark with their scent, particularly around common feeding areas. This practice allows individual group members to recognize each other.

The Ring-Tailed Lemur

The image of the popular ring-tailed lemur almost always appears in the tourist pamphlets that portray Madagascar as the "enchanted island-continent."

The thick, grayish pink coat, the black mask surrounding its lively eyes, the pointy snout, and the long tail encircled by white and black rings evoke a loving feeling in the observer. It is not accidental that the ring-tailed lemur has been selected as a character of Madagascar cartoons. Its objective is to entertain Madagascar children and to teach them love and respect for nature. There have been many scientific books written on the ring-tailed lemur.

The ring-tailed lemur marks its territory in a peculiar way. In addition to scented glands in the genital area, the male has two types of glands on one side of its front legs. The ring-tailed lemur spreads the scents of these glands on the leaves and branches within its territory. If it is confronted by another animal, it stands up on its hind legs and rubs the tail against the glands of the front legs. It then changes posture by standing on its four legs, swinging the scented tail towards its rival.

According to some scientists, the continuous marking of the territory is intended to reduce aggressiveness among competing groups of lemurs which occupy bordering areas. In the opinion of other researchers, the conspicuous color of the tail and the behavior are signs that indicate the "moods" of the animal.

During the mating period the females are sexually receptive and mate with any adult male in the group. Sometimes they mate even with younger males, if adults are lacking. Births occur in the fall, and the young grow rapidly. Fifteen days after birth the tiny lemurs are already capable of riding on their mother's back, or if possible, on the back of another female or young group member. They become independent one month after birth.

The ring-tailed lemurs are active only during the day, and they rest during the hottest hours. They spend a great part of their time exploring the ground or basking in the sun in areas of the forest where the trees are more scattered. During small excursions, they leap with agility from one tree to another in search of food. Their food consists of tamarind seeds and buds, tender acacia twigs, leaves and fruits of the native trees, and other substances. At times they feed on larvae and insects, especially large cicadas. They drink in specific areas during their wanderings, such as

along riverbanks or at a water hole. Usually, however, they satisfy their thirst by licking dew from leaves.

Two additional lemurs worth mentioning are the weasel lemur and the ruffed lemur. The weasel lemur is common in the wet forests of eastern Madagascar. It is characterized by a slightly shortened snout and a dark gray coat. The ruffed lemur has an extraordinary silky coat with black and white bands. It never leaves the tree environment, where it marks its territory by rubbing branches with the scent from a neck gland. Another sign of territoriality is conveyed through a powerful chorus of screeches. These calls often are answered by screeches from nearby areas.

The sportive lemur is nocturnal and lives in the trees of the eastern forests. These lemurs are known for their large eyes and round and protruding ears. They reach a length of between 20 and 28 inches (50 to 70 cm). Their diet consists almost exclusively of leaves. For this reason their intestines are long. The considerable length of this lemur's intestines enable it to digest these leaves.

The sifaka and the endrina are two interesting species of wooly lemurs. The sifakas have been classified according to numerous geographical groups. The body colors of these groups vary between white, reddish, and brown. These colors often appear with beautiful combinations. Sifakas are 18 inches (45 cm) long not counting the tail, which alone may measures 22 inches (55 cm). These lemurs are active mainly during the day and live on trees. They feed on leaves, flowers, and tender buds, which they eat with their hands.

Certain scientists have observed that, unlike monkeys, the sifakas are not able to use their hands to gather food which has fallen on the ground. They grasp food first with their mouths and then they chew it by holding it with the fingers and the palm of the hand. Both hands and feet are particularly adapted to tree life. Movements on the ground and on the branches are made by a series of acrobatic jumps. The body is in a semi-erect position while jumping. The tail serves as a balancer as the hands grasp the most flexible branches during its forward movements.

Unlike other lemurs, such as the ring-tailed lemur, the sifaka can also be found outside the forest environment. Often they venture into woodlands dominated by thorny plants. Here they climb with agility (and without hurting themselves) over tree trunks covered by sharp thorns. A rich variety of communicative and warning screeches characterizes the calls of the sifaka.

Opposite page: A lemur is discovered in the Berenty Reserve, near Fort Dauphin. The Madagascan lemurs include twenty-six well-known living species, grouped in five families. Twelve extinct species have been identified from fossilized remains. Some species have disappeared during the last one thousand years. Many of these extinct lemurs existed when the first humans colonized Madagascar. Almost certainly, the disappearance of these animals was caused by extensive hunting and the destruction of their natural habitat.

The endrina lemura *(top)* is the largest living lemur. It prefers leaves, buds and fruits and is active only during the day. It spends a large part of its life in the trees. Only rarely does it descend to the ground. Its social life takes place in small family groups consisting of five to eight animals. Each group controls a territory of 2,150 to 10,764 sq. feet (200 to 1,000 sq. m) of forest and undergrowth. The ruffed lemur with its elegant black-and-white coat *(bottom)*, is a good climber and is active at sunset and in the evening. During the day it rests or basks in the sun.

The screech of the endrina is much louder and more impressive. This is the largest living lemur. In the moist forests of the eastern mountain slopes one can hear the whining of the endrinas, which has a very human quality. This sound, which can be heard up to a distance of about 1 mile (2 km), is answered by the sounds of other distant endrinas scattered throughout the forest.

The endrina is not easily seen. However, by following its call, it is possible to find a small group of two to five endrinas hanging from the branches of the highest trees in the forest. The extraordinary power of the endrina's call is attributed to the presence of a well-developed throat. This particular feature cannot be found in any other species of lemurs. The endrina's large size (almost 28 inches/70 cm in length), the presence of only a stump of a tail, and its almost human call, have inspired many legends among the Madagascar people. According to these legends, the endrina is one of their ancestors and for this reason it is respected and never hunted.

The Aye-Aye

An overview of Madagascar lemurs would not be complete without mentioning the extremely rare aye-aye. At one time, scientists considered the aye-aye a type of squirrel, because of its bushy tail and long front teeth, which grow continuously. Actually, the aye-aye is a lemur. It is about the same size of the ring-tailed lemur, and it has large round eyes and a thick coat of rough, brownish hair with a sprinkling of white. The rather short snout is surrounded by two large, bare and movable ears and by the conspicuous hair of its eyebrows.

The aye-aye has peculiarly-shaped forelimbs. The long fingers, with the exception of the thumb, end in claws. The third finger of the hand is extremely thin, almost skeletal.

The aye-aye is fond of insect larvae. It can climb with great agility on trees and palms, where it builds a spherical nest made of leaves and twigs. The nest where the aye-aye rests during the day has a side entrance. By using its extremely sensitive senses of hearing and smell, the aye-aye carefully combs through the dead branches of trees or large fruits with holes in search of larvae. As it locates the prey within these cavities, the aye-aye carves out the bark and wood using its sharp front teeth to expose the cavity. It then puts its middle finger into the hole, turning it around and around until it is finally able to pull out the larvae. The prey

The aye-aye is the rarest pre-ape in the world. It is active at night and its diet consists mainly of insects, although it prefers the soft pulp and milk of the coconut. The aye-aye is able to pull out the coconut meat with its long, thin fingers after having chewed on the hard coconut shell. The aye-aye represents a unique case of a mammal occupying an ecological niche typically occupied by birds (such as the woodpecker) which do not inhabit Madagascar.

is eaten immediately and the aye-aye promptly resumes its hunt.

Unfortunately, this animal has been hunted by the natives for two reasons. It damages coconut plantations and it is also believed to be an omen of misfortune in native villages. The continuous devastation of its natural habitat has been the most critical factor in the decline of its population. This animal has now reached the point of being considered one of the rarest mammals in the world.

BIRDS, AMPHIBIANS AND REPTILES

Birds

Although Madagascar has a relatively low number of birds, it has a large number of native species. Of the 238 known species of birds inhabiting the island, more than half are natives of Madagascar. Furthermore, there are similarities with the African birds and to a lesser degree with the Asian birds. The total absence of certain groups of birds which are well-represented in Asia and Africa is rather peculiar.

Madagascar does, however, host a number of birds of uncertain origins that are completely different from the rest of the birds found here. This fact leads to the theory that these birds may be the last descendants of ancient species, which may have been common in other continents at one time, but later disappeared. Perhaps they were replaced by birds with a better ecological adaptation. The giant elephant-bird (a distant relative of the ostriches and cassowaries) is a good example. This extinct bird reached the incredible height of 10 feet (3 m). During the Cretaceous period this flightless, primitive bird must have entered the territory of Madagascar by walking from other continents before they became separated.

In the absence of predators, the elephant-bird was able to survive by occupying the space which was not used by the herbivores. It browsed in the grasslands of the extreme south, and had no real competitors. Fossilized remains and the shells of enormous eggs can still be found in the dunes of the south.

Other primitive and mysterious birds that arrived in Madagascar by flight were the mesites. These native birds can still be seen in Madagascar, though they have become very rare. Their plumage is somewhat similar to that of the herons. Their beaks are either pointed or curved and their plumage is speckled with a brown color. They inhabit the forests and woodlands of the east and west where they thrive on the leaf-covered soil. In these zones they roost on short bushes.

Although relatively poor in the number of species, the birds of Madagascar have been able to spread evenly into many environments and have been able to harmoniously adapt in those habitats. Accordingly, certain evolutionary lines of birds have been able to develop in different ways. The origin of these groups can be traced back to a common ancestor. Typical examples are the native vanga-shrikes and the peculiar long-tailed cuckoos, or couas.

Opposite page: The hammerhead bird is a heron that is common in the moist environments of both Madagascar and the African continent south of the Sahara Desert.

89

The coua evolved from an Asian ancestor. There are a dozen couas in Madagascar. In the course of evolution, these birds have occupied several types of ecological niches which correspond basically to two categories. Some couas are exclusively tree dwellers. Other larger couas instead prefer the ground, like the European pheasant. Their round wings are not particularly suited for flying. They rummage on the ground in search of insects and snails.

The Delalande coua is another ground dweller. This bird, which may well be extinct, has beautiful white and reddish feathers. The last time it was spotted was in 1834. Its strong, curved beak served a specific purpose related to its special diet. With its beak it was capable of breaking the shell of large snails which it found among the dead leaves of the northeastern forests of Madagascar.

Even more evident is the evolutionary variety of the vanga-shrikes, which are perching birds related to the European shrikes. Several species are widespread in the various ecosystems of Madagascar. They are insect-eaters which originated and evolved to their present forms from a common ancestor. They differ in their diet and the manner in which they seek food.

Some species of vanga-shrikes have large, hooked beaks and feed on small reptiles, amphibians, and also small mammals. The orioles ambush their insect prey and other lively, multicolored birds search the twigs at the top of trees for insects. Falculia birds with long, curved beaks carefully search the branches of the baobab tree for larvae, insects, and lizards. Together with the aye-aye, the falculia has been able to exploit the empty ecological niche which elsewhere would have been filled by the woodpecker.

The coral-billed nuthatch is a small bird with gray-blue feathers and a reddish beak. Its behavior is similar to that of the European woodpecker. It climbs tree trunks with a spiral-like movement, in search of larvae and insects.

Other typical birds are the ground-rollers, which are a native group of roller birds. These birds are distant relatives of the sea jays. They are common mostly in the thick rain forests, where they search the bushes for insects. The most peculiar among them is the long-tailed ground-roller. The tail of this bird is twice as long as its body. It is active at dusk and at night and lives in the subdesert woodlands of the southwest. It makes its nest in holes which it digs in the soil.

Four species of asities have evolved in the primary forests of Madagascar. The asities birds have a velvety plumage and are similar to the sunbirds and small pittas.

Along with these birds of mysterious origin there are other birds which are related to species inhabiting the African continent. However, despite their similarities, these birds do not belong to the same species.

An example is the fruit-eating pigeon. This bird has olive-green feathers which camouflage it when roosting amid the leaves of trees. Several metallic-colored sunbirds, the inseparable lovebird parrots, and the multicolored king-fisher have their closest relatives in Africa, across the Mozambique Channel.

The hawks of Madagascar, which prey on lemurs and other vertebrates, probably evolved from African ancestors. The hammerhead bird is very common in Madagascar and in Africa. This bird did not evolve in different groups on this island; its arrival in Madagascar is probably a fairly recent event. On the other hand, quite a few Madagascar birds represent the descendants of birds which at one time originated in Asia but never colonized the African continent.

The small black-and-white thrush is a close relative of the Indian and Indonesian dyal. This bird can also be found in the Seychelles Islands.

The dollarbird is a noisy roller bird with beautiful brown, red, and violet feathers. It is easy to spot in the forest. In fact, this bird prefers to rest on the tips of branches or dead trunks, where it produces a series of ear-piercing noises. Its mating season in Madagascar lasts from December to January. It then migrates to Africa, crossing the Mozambique Channel around March. It nests in tree cavities. Both male and female do not hesitate to aggressively attack any intruder that approaches the nest.

The bulbul bird also originated in Asia. This bird is well-known for its explosive calls which it makes from the tops of trees. Other "Oriental" birds are the small but belligerent black drongo, which has a forked tail and a beautiful crest. There is a group of related species of black or grayish brown parrots that are typically found in Madagascar, the Comoro and the Seychelles Islands. Most probably these birds had an Asian origin. It is hard to miss them because of their loud and repetitive screeches, which echo through the forest starting at early dawn.

Another group of very interesting birds is the migratory birds. These birds live in Madagascar but migrate to their land of origin in certain seasons. Such is the case of the large sea jay with brown-violet feathers and a strong, bright yellow beak. In the fall (March to May) this migratory bird crosses the Mozambique Channel to winter in eastern Africa. This is another noisy bird of the Madagascar forest. It prefers the tips of branches or dead trunks from where it makes a series of deafening cries. One can also observe the queen falcon.

Amphibians and Reptiles

Peculiar native species of amphibians and reptiles abound in Madagascar. According to recent studies, Madagascar numbers at least 128 species of amphibians and 260 reptile species. Ninety five percent of these are native species. Despite this rich variety of species, one might immediately notice that the family groups represented are relatively few if compared to the other groups of native land animals. The number of snake families, for example, shows a remarkable imbalance compared to that of the neighboring continents of Africa and Asia.

As was mentioned earlier, many animals arrived on the coast of Madagascar by means of floating vegetation. Others perhaps swam to the island. The true frogs were the only amphibians that were able to reach the island. The toads, tree frogs, salamanders, and the legless amphibians never made it to Madagascar.

The true frogs evolved into numerous forms, adapting to each type of environment. In Madagascar certain frogs have evolved special extensions on their legs with which they dig shelters in the drier soils. The majority of frogs, however, are found in moister forest habitats.

In addition to aquatic environments, numerous species of frogs may be found in other micro-environments that offer protection from evaporation. Water-filled cavities of the bamboo plant, shelters offered by rotting trunks, rock crevices, and leaf bases of epiphytes (plants that grow on other plants for support but not for food) are examples.

The life cycle is short in many species of frogs, reflecting changeable and unpredictable environmental conditions. For example, certain frogs which live in holes or under moss rapidly develop from tadpoles to adults. Other frogs lay foamy masses of eggs in dry areas among the plants which arch over the swamps. From these plants the hatched tadpoles fall into the water.

The chameleon has a long, retractable tongue for catching insects that it ambushes from tree branches. It can rotate both eyes independently from each other in order to maximize its visual range.

The crocodile is the fiercest reptile of Madagascar. It survives in certain rivers and lakes, such as the Anivorane, which are considered sacred. The animal is regarded as a taboo (an object believed to be sacred or cursed by natives). Oxen are fed to crocodiles each year during popular festivals. The geckos, chameleons, and iguanas are some of the significant saurian reptiles on the island. There are no monitor, agamid, or lacertid lizards, which, instead, are common in Asia and Africa. The existence of two species of iguanas in the isolation of Madagascar is a real mystery. This group is well-represented in the Americas and to a small degree in Oceania. However, the iguanas are completely absent in Africa.

According to certain scientists, the African agamid lizards may have pushed the iguanas out of the African continent. This could have taken place during the course of their evolution in the middle of the Tertiary period, and it could have led to the forceful exile of the iguanas into Madagascar. Naturally, this is only a theory.

One of the Madagascar iguanas has preserved features that are definitely primitive. This reptile thrives in sandy areas and measures about 12 inches (30 cm). The males display bright colors during the mating season and defend their territory from rivals. The other iguana includes a few species that inhabit trees or rocky environments.

The most peculiar gecko lizard on Madagascar is the leaftailed gecko, a native tree dweller common in the eastern forests. It is less than 12 inches (30 cm) long and has a flat body. It can camouflage itself among the bark, the lichens, and the tree trunks where it lives. Its skin folds, wide, leafy tail, and round eyes are similar to a small crocodile.

There are many species of small day geckos that inhabit trees. They have bright green colors, red spots, and white and yellow stripes. Particular types can be found in the Mascarene, Comoro, and Seychelles Islands.

The list of lizards would not be complete without mentioning the chameleons and the stump-tailed chameleons. These are well known reptiles originally from East Africa. However, two-thirds of the species that have been studied can be found exclusively in Madagascar.

The various Madagascar chameleons are characterized by a small head helmet, a nose protuberance, or swelling, and dimensions which vary from 4 to 26 inches (10 to 68 cm). They are common in any environment where there are bushes from which they can ambush insects.

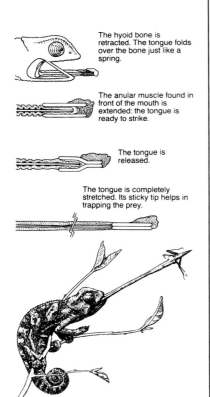

The hyoid bone is retracted. The tongue folds over the bone just like a spring.

The anular muscle found in front of the mouth is extended: the tongue is ready to strike.

The tongue is released.

The tongue is completely stretched. Its sticky tip helps in trapping the prey.

The snakes of Madagascar are another case of strange geographical distribution. The boa family is common in the Americas but is absent in Africa. In Madagascar it is represented by two native species, which are mostly peaceful. One is a large boa up to 6 feet (180 cm) long with an elegant brown body and light spots. It thrives along the moist edges of creeks and swamps where it feeds on small vertebrate animals. Unfortunately, these reptiles are on their way to extinction due to extensive hunting and the destruction of their habitats.

There are other native snakes that are not well-known. One of these snakes co-exists with ant colonies and is of great interest to zoologists. None of the snakes mentioned thus far are poisonous or dangerous to humans.

Another reptile threatened by extinction is the land tortoise. Some species of turtles are now found only in restricted dry bush areas of the Antandroy territory in southern Madagascar. One of these turtles is a beautiful animal, 24 inches (60 cm) long, with a high, dark shell decorated with yellow stripes. The natives are fond of this animal. During rainy periods it can be seen near their vil-

A dwarf chameleon ventures over a leaf in the humid forest of the Perinet reserve. This is the smallest of the chameleon species, native to Madagascar.

The most sensational experience for any underwater photographer is to come across the fabled coelacanth. This fish, once thought to have been extinct seventy million years ago, has been rediscovered off the coast of Madagascar and the Comoro Islands. According to scientists, this living fossil can be found only in the deepest waters of the Mozambique Channel.

lages. In the past, this large turtle found a natural shelter in the thorny cactus fences which the natives built around their properties. However, for the past few decades the cacti have been destroyed by infestations of scale insects. Their shelters have thus been destroyed.

Another similar turtle, Geochelone yniphora, can be found in the dry sakalav territory of Northwest Madagascar. This is perhaps one of the rarest turtles in the world. Efforts are being made today to breed these animals in captivity for later reintroduction into their native habitat.

The Seas

The seas surrounding Madagascar are full of amazing organisms which deserve special attention. In contrast with the Madagascan land animals, the marine animal life does not display a high number of native species or unusual biological forms.

Because of Madagascar's position in the southwestern part of the Indian Ocean, its coast is bathed by numerous currents. These currents carry the most diverse animal and plant forms from the Indian and Pacific oceans.

Long stretches of mangrove swamps are commonly found along the Madagascar coast. The environment of the mangrove swamps is constantly subject to the rhythm of the tides. These areas are full of mollusks, shellfish, strange fish, crabs, and amphibians. On the western coast, in places such as Tular, there are dazzling strips of limestone sand contrasting with the intense turquoise color of the sea and the sky, and with the dark green of the interior vegetation.

Along the coast there are reefs consisting of thousands of colonies of madrepore corals of various sizes and shapes. Sea life abounds around these branching coral structures. The sea animals include shellfish, starfish, sea urchins, and colorful parrot and butterfly fish.

Dangerous sharks also inhabit these waters. Often they come close to the shore or follow rivers upstream for many miles. One can still encounter the majestic sea turtle. Unfortunately, they are becoming rarer due to extensive hunting. The sea cow is also becoming rare. It is found along sandy shores and estuaries. The survival of this mammal is in jeopardy throughout the Indian Ocean. This is due to the extensive hunting by humans for their flesh, oil, and skin.

ARCHIPELAGOES OF THE MALAGASY REGION

A few archipelagoes in the Indian Ocean are like interesting laboratories because they have once been centers of evolution. Although these islands belong to the region of Madagascar, these areas must be treated separately for biological and geographical reasons. They are the Comoro, the Mascarene and the Seychelles Islands.

The Comoro Islands

Located at the northern extremity of the Mozambique Channel, the Comoro group is an archipelago of volcanic and coral origin.

These islands are very similar to Madagascar from a geographical and biological perspective. There are four major islands: the Great Comoro, with a surface of 443 square miles (1,148 sq. km), is located 174 miles (280 km) from the African coast. Its volcano, the Karthala, reaches a height of 7,743 feet (2,360 m) at distances which vary between 25 and 43 miles (40 and 70 km).

There are also three other large islands: Moheli, with an area of 112 sq. miles (290 sq. km); Anjouan, with an area of 139 sq. miles (359 sq. km); and Mayotte, with an area of 144 sq. miles (374 sq. km). These islands have a typical monsoon climate with seasonal rainfall from November to April (which is the summer of the Southern Hemisphere). During the same period hurricanes can also occur.

The soil is very fertile and a great part of the island has been converted to agriculture. Vanilla, pepper, bananas, ylang-ylang, cocoa, and pineapples are widely cultivated in the islands.

The coasts are bordered by coral reefs, beaches of limestone or black volcanic sand, or by muddy mangrove swamps. Further inland are agricultural areas and rich forests such trees as the acagiu, containing and the palisander.

Madagascar and the Comoro Islands are inhabited by certain lemurs, which have evolved into native species. The tenrec is also common as well as a type of flying fox with a brownish black coat. Among the native birds are black parrots, white and blue pigeons, and forest sunbirds. Different kinds of curol kingfishers are commonly found in woodland areas.

The ocean waters of the Comoro Islands are famous for the abundance of fish as well as animals dependent on the coral reef. In the waters around Anjouan, prehistoric coelacanth fish has occasionally been caught.

Opposite page: A palm tree is photographed at Praslin in the Seychelles Islands.

The interesting geological phenomenon of the "Colored Earth" is seen in Mauritius.

The Mascarene Islands

The Mascarene Islands include a group of three main islands of volcanic origin located at 19° 40′ and 21° 0′ latitude south (barely north of the Tropic of Capricorn) and at 63° 25′ longitude east.

The islands are about 1,000 miles (1,600 km) from Madagascar and are usually affected by southeast winds in addition to the south-equatorial current coming from an east-west direction. Reunion is the largest island, with an area of 970 sq. miles (2,512 sq. km) and a maximum elevation of 10,070 feet (3,069 m). Mauritius has an area of about 1,583 sq. miles (1,865 sq. km). Its highest peak reaches 4,101

feet (1,250 m). Rodrigues, several hundred miles east of Mauritius, has an area of 42 sq. miles (109 sq. km).

The climate of the Mascarene Islands is characterized by frequent rainfall during the summer season. From January to April the archipelago is hit by violent hurricanes and heavy rainfall.

The interior of Mauritius was once covered by bamboo and ebony forests. Today it is cultivated with sugar cane, tobacco, tea and pineapple. The forests of Rodrigues have also been replaced by coffee, rice and tobacco plantations.

Fifteen miles from Mauritius there is a group of small islands. The largest of these islands is Round Island with an area of about 6 sq. miles (15.5 sq. km). Round Island is now deserted and its plant cover has been almost completely destroyed by soil erosion. The erosion is primarily caused by hurricanes and by the overgrazing of goats and rabbits, which were introduced in the nineteenth century. The original forest of native palms can be found only in a few areas. Unfortunately, interesting native species of snakes, geckos, and skinks will become extinct as the result of the disappearance of their natural habitat.

In the island of Reunion the high mountain terrain has encouraged the evolution of several plant habitats. Some of these habitats still exist today in spite of great changes brought about by the natives. Along the east coast is a forest typical of humid areas with low elevations. Past this forest is another type of forest which is more characteristic of humid areas with medium-high elevations—roughly 5,500 feet (1,675 m). Above this level, an alpine-type of low vegetation appears. At higher elevations, plants are scattered and the underlying rock is exposed. The west coast of Reunion is somewhat drier.

The only native Mascarene mammals are the flying foxes. These animals are on the verge of extinction in the islands of Rodrigues and Mauritius.

The Mascarene Islands are also known for their many native bird species. The birds here were able to evolve in isolation, undisturbed by predators and competitors. The islands are famous for several types of dodo birds that once inhabited them. Each island had one representative of these flightless species: Mauritius had the dodo, Reunion had the white dodo, and Rodrigues had the solitary dodo.

The population of dodo birds began its decline to extinction in the seventeenth century, after the colonization of the Mascarene Islands by navigators and pioneers.

Top right: This coral lagoon, known as the Lagon d'Alphonse, in the Amirante Islands of the Seychelles.

Bottom: The giant tortoise is one of the largest species of land turtle found on any island. Aldabra Island is an important refuge for this animal.

The Seychelles Islands

The Seychelles is a group of about ninety islands. They lie north of Madagascar and are about 1,000 miles (1,609 km) east of the African coast. The islands are spread over abour 400,000 sq. mi. (1,035,995 sq. km). The archipelago has four main islands: Mahe, Silhouette, Praslin and La Digue. Farther north one finds two islets of coral origin: Denis Island and Bird Island.

The climate is tropical with one dry season. The seas are choppy from May to October, when the southwest monsoon arrives. From December to March the weather improves considerably; the sea becomes calm and rainfall increases. Fortunately, the Seychelles Islands are outside the general area affected by the hurricanes.

The birds of the Seychelles Islands number various native species, although many of these species are on the verge of extinction.

Noteworthy among these are the flycatcher of paradise, the copsic (now found only on Fregate and Aride), the fruit-eating pigeon, and the black parrots. Fortunately, a few reserves and sanctuaries have been created to protect these interesting native animals.

Rare specimens of the giant land turtle still survive in the Seychelles Islands. Once very numerous, these reptiles were exterminated by humans. These long-lived turtles can reach a length of 6.6 feet (2 m) and weigh 550 lbs. (250 kg). An important group of these animals can be found on Aldabra Island, where they are carefully monitored.

GUIDE TO AREAS OF NATURAL INTEREST

Southern Africa, Madagascar, and their archipelagos abound with interesting natural areas such as reserves, national parks and sanctuaries. The following pages will present only a few of the many protected areas.

Further information may be found directly at these locations, at least in the majority of cases. Contacting the various administrators of individual parks in advance for reserving cabins or campsites is recommended. The visitor should also seek information on park opening periods as well as information on vaccinations and other health precautions. In fact, in certain areas visits are not possible during the hottest and wettest periods. For example, the Etosha National Park is closed from November to the end of February during the rainy season.

It is also advisable to plan the visit during the local school season in order to avoid crowds and to enjoy a more peaceful vacation.

Photography fans should obviously remember to take along film since it may sometime not be possible to find film in these areas. When available, it is far more expensive than in Europe or America.

Obviously, it is important to follow the rules and regulations prescribed by the park authorities.

Madagascar requires permits for visits to parks and reserves which are available from the Ministry of Water and Forests in Antananarivo. There are two types of parks and reserves on the island. Each type enforces its own rules and regulations. Therefore, whoever travels for reasons that do not particularly relate to tourism should obtain information ahead of time.

The visitor should also keep in mind that Madagascar strictly prohibits the export not only of live animals, but also of animal parts. For example, seashells or empty shells cannot be taken abroad.

Opposite page: An eagle rests on top of a dead tree in the Etosha National Park. Weaverbirds have built their intricate, large nests on the branches of the same tree. This eagle is a rather common bird of prey in all arid areas.

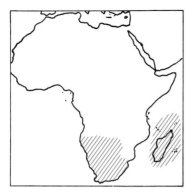

The map shows the African regions and nearby islands covered in this book. The most interesting national parks and nature reserves are also charted.

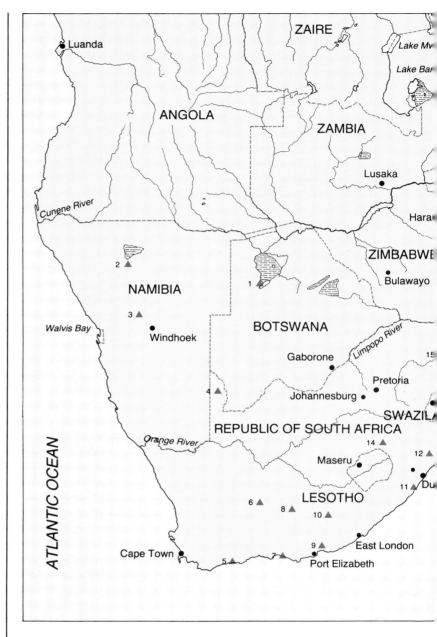

BOTSWANA

Moremi (1)

This reserve covers an area of 1,125 sq. miles (2,914 sq. km). It was established to protect the Okavango environment. The large plateau is rich in mopane forests, tree ferns, and very clear streams. Several habitats offer protection to buffalo, lions, elephants, and various species of antelopes and baboons. Bird life is very rich, particularly the aquatic species. The reserve is open during the entire year.

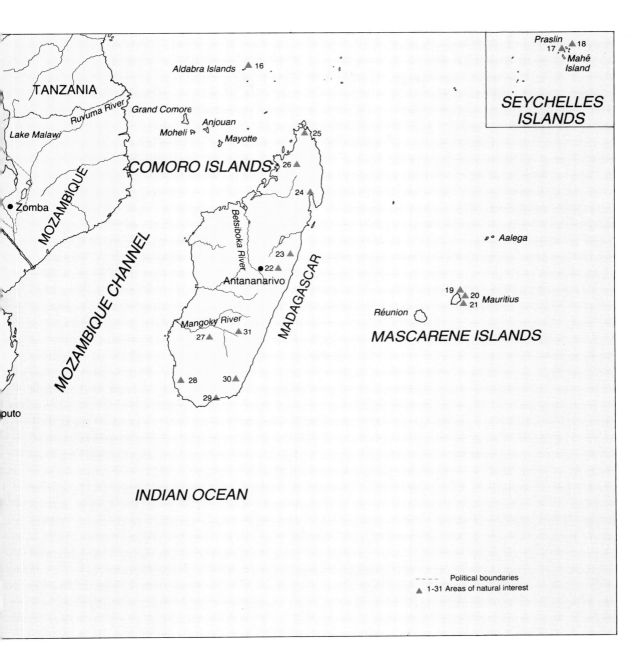

Aldabra Islands ▲ 16

TANZANIA

Ruvuma River

Lake Malawi

Grand Comore
Anjouan
Moheli
Mayotte

COMORO ISLANDS

Zomba

MOZAMBIQUE

26 ▲

24 ▲

25 ▲

Betsiboka River

23 ▲

22 ▲

Antananarivo

MADAGASCAR

MOZAMBIQUE CHANNEL

Mangoky River

27 ▲   ▲ 31

28 ▲

30 ▲

29 ▲

Praslin ▲ 18
17 ▲
Mahé
Island

SEYCHELLES
ISLANDS

Aalega

19 ▲
20
21 ▲   Mauritius

Réunion

MASCARENE ISLANDS

puto

INDIAN OCEAN

- - - - Political boundaries
▲ 1-31 Areas of natural interest

NAMIBIA

Etosha (2)

Founded in 1907, Namibia's second-largest park covers an area of 8,878 sq. miles (23,000 sq. km). Etosha is located about 310 miles (500 km) north of Windhoek. Its center is occupied by a large, flat, desert-like area which fills with water at the beginning of the summer rainfall season. Its waters are full of organisms which represent an important source of food for flamingos and other species of birds.

Large herbivores are also numerous, such as elephants, black rhinoceroses, giraffes, and antelopes. At one time the wildebeest could be seen while making long migrations in search of grasses. Today, however, their movements are hindered by park fences, which have resulted in a sharp reduction of the herds.

There are also numerous carnivores, such as the brown hyena, and over three hundred species of birds. Three campgrounds with good facilities offer comfortable accommodations.

Namib-Naukluft (3)

This is Namibia's largest park. It was established in 1979 by merging three small parks. It covers an area of 9,033 sq. miles (23,401 sq. km). The Kuiseb River divides the area into two sections. Toward the south there is a wide expanse of sand with some of the highest dunes in the world. Toward the west there is Walvis Bay, an important bird sanctuary containing over seventy species of birds. In the east, the Naukluft region has spectacular mountains, beautiful valleys, and numerous perennial springs. Gemsbok and springbok antelopes, ostriches, and mountain zebras are among the most typical animals. Several species of insects inhabit the dunes, as well as the barking gecko lizard. The park is open throughout the year. However, from October to March it is very hot. During these months special permits are required for visiting certain areas. Campgrounds only have essential services.

SOUTH AFRICA

Kalahari Gemsbok (4)

This national park covers an area of 3,702 square miles (9,591 sq. km) in the northwesternmost part of South Africa, near the border with Namibia and Botswana. This is an interesting semi-desert region located between the dry riverbeds of the Nossob and Auob rivers.

The typical red Kalahari Desert dunes with scattered grasses and trees can be found between these two rivers. Various types of acacia trees prevail along the riverbeds. A unique plant, the tsamma, represents an important food and water source for the desert animal, especially for the gemsbok which are fond of it.

The dunes are inhabited by enormous herds of wildebeest, springbok, and eland. In addition there are lions, cheetahs, leopards, and hyenas. Here one can also find two hundred species of birds, including the weavers. These birds are well-known because of their enormous nests.

Bontebok (5)

This national park is located a few miles from Swellendam, in an area of 11 sq. miles (28 sq. km) on the slopes of the Langeberg Mountains. The park was created in 1960 to protect the bontebok antelope, which at that time was on the verge of extinction. Today, three hundred specimens of bontebok live in this area together with other species of antelope. In the spring (September to November), when a large number of plants blossom, the park acquires a bright and colorful appearance.

Among the luxuriant vegetation which numbers 460 species, the most common plants are the heaths, gladiolus, and three kinds of silk-oaks. Along the banks of the Breede River are various types of trees, including the yellowwood. Other local species are the boekenhout, milkwood, and sweet thorn trees.

The park hosts almost two hundred species of birds, including the secretary bird, several types of sunbirds, ospreys, ptarmigans, and a great variety of reptiles and amphibians.

Karroo (6)

In 1979, an area of 68 sq. miles (177 sq. km) in the interior of the Great Karroo was declared a national park. The dry and semi-desert scenery is characterized by mountains, flatland, and mesas. The scattered vegetation is typical of the Karroo and covers the entire territory. It consists primarily of low shrubs, perennial grasses, and thorny bushes.

The park is inhabited by about fifty species of mammals, including the mountain zebra, gemsbok, red hartebeest, wildebeest, springbok, kudu, and jackal.

There are no real roads in the park. To visit the park one must follow the Springbok hiking trail for 25 miles (41 km).

Tsitsikamma Forest (7)

This park, which covers an area of 1.5 sq. miles (4 sq. km) has been created to protect the luxuriant vegetation typical of the southeastern area of Cape Province. The temperate climate and abundant rainfall promote the growth of a thick forest. The yellowwood tree prevails among the numerous tree species, sometimes reaching a height of 165 feet (50 m). Other common trees are the stinkwood, Cape chestnut, and assegai.

The forest is crossed by several trails of great biological interest. From these trails one can observe giant trees and numerous species of forest birds such as the Knysna touraco and the narina trogon. A rest area with camping accommodations is located near the park.

A nyala wades in a marshy area of the
Mkuzi Nature Reserve. From blinds set
up near drinking holes, visitors can
watch herbivores and predators in their
natural environment.

Tsitsikamma Coastal (8)

This national park runs along the southeastern coast of Cape Province for approximately 50 miles (80 km).

A thick vegetation covers the steep hills in the interior and stretches all the way to the ocean. These hills form dips, slopes, and rocky beaches along the seashore. The undergrowth is dense and rich in heaths, lichens,and podocarp trees.

Numerous mammals of small and medium size live in this area. Dolphins and whales can be easily seen in the ocean water. Along the beaches,there are over thirty species of seabirds. The well-known Otter Trail is in the interior of the park. Part of this trail runs alongside the ocean, while another part runs alongside the Storms River. It takes about four to five days to cover this beautiful area.

At the center of the park is a modern and well-organized campground. Here, both simple cabins and luxury chalets are available for accommodations.

Addo Elephant (9)

Because of extensive hunting, around 1920 the number of elephants in the eastern part of Cape Province declined to only eleven animals. What was once considered a subspecies of the African elephant became endangered. The Addo National Park was established in 1931 to protect this endangered species. Today, the park shelters over one hundred elephants in an area of 33 sq. miles (86 sq. km). The environment consists of a dense woodland with a number of species of trees, among which is the spekboom, a favorite food of the elephant. Kudus, buffalos, black rhinoceroses, and hartebeests are among the inhabitants of the park. There is only one well-organized campground in the park.

Mountain Zebra (10)

This national park covers an area of 25 sq. miles (65 sq. km) and is located in the Great Karroo of Cape Province. It was established in 1937 with the objective of protecting the mountain zebra. By 1937 mountain zebras had been hunted almost to the verge of extinction. Today, the survival of the species has been ensured, and the park shelters at least two hundred specimens. This is the maximum number that can be supported by the natural resources of the park. Excess zebras are transferred to other areas of their old environment according to a repopulation plan.

Next to the zebra, wildebeest, eland, springbok and other antelopes live in the vast plateau. There are over two hundred species of birds, including eagles.

The somewhat hilly countryside varies from a dry veld with succulent plants (typical of the Karroo) to a more moist grassland toward the east. In the park, good accommodations in a restored colonial-style house or in comfortable chalets near the campsite can be found.

Umfolozi (11)

This protected area is important because of the great number of white rhinoceroses which inhabit it. In fact, this is the largest group of rhinos (about nine hundred specimens) in existence. It is possible to cross the reserve by a trail which runs for 298 miles (480 km). This travel plan can be accomplished in three days and it covers the wildest and least accessible areas. Here one can observe various animals such as the buffalo, black rhino, zebra, giraffe, lion, leopard, cheetah, and several species of antelope.

Mkuzi (12)

This reserve covers an area of 10 sq. miles (25 sq. km) and is located at the foot of the Lebombo Mountain Chain. Here, the environment changes from dense woodlands to a savanna. There are three observation points near water holes where animals gather to drink. From these points one can observe numerous animals, including black and white rhinoceroses, giraffes, zebras, and numerous species of antelopes. Among the carnivores, there are leopards and cheetahs. It is possible to visit the park by following a three-day trail accompanied by guides. One campground offers good facilities.

St. Lucia (13)

The coastal reservation of St. Lucia includes a large lake bordering the seashore. This is a fisherman's paradise. Many hippopotamuses, crocodiles, and antelopes inhabit this area. In addition to the usual guided hikes along the trails, boat excursions can be made from St. Lucia's estuary. Comfortable accommodations are available at the two campsites or in the two hut villages.

Golden Gate Highland (14)

Established in 1963, this national park is famous for its rich animal life and for its breathtaking scenery. It is located northeast of the Free State of Orange between the slopes of the Maluti mountains. The altitude ranges between 6,208 and 9,088 feet (1,892 and 2,770 m), and the park covers an area of 18.5 sq. miles (48 sq. km). The majestic mountains surrounding the park reflect a characteristic golden light, which gives this park its name. In the winter the climate is quite cold. It snows often, the waterfalls freeze, and the temperature may reach 10°F (-12°C). At high elevations the climate and vegetation (consisting mainly of grasses) give the environment a completely different appearance from that of other South African parks.

Zebras and various species of antelope inhabit this area, as well as the black eagle.

There are two tourist villages. The largest, Brandwag, offers luxury accommodations and recreational activities.

Kruger (15)

The largest national park of South Africa is located about 250 miles (400 km) northeast of the city of Johannesburg. The park, established in 1926, covers an area of 7,720 sq. miles (20,000 sq. km). The altitude varies from 660 feet (200 m) in the eastern part to 2,953 feet (900 m) in the southwestern part. It is crossed by large rivers along which a luxuriant forest grows. In some sections, there is savanna with acacia, mopane, and marula trees.

This park is particularly important for the great variety of animals which live there. One hundred and twenty-two species of mammals roam the park, including predators such as lions, cheetahs, and hyenas. Many herbivores are also found in the park, for example buffalo, elephants, rhinoceroses, giraffes, and hippopotamuses. The rare tsessebe and the horse antelope, in addition to the more numerous kudus and impalas, should also be mentioned. The important bird life is represented by over four hundred species.

Inside the park there are fourteen villages, offering various types of accommodations, many of which are very comfortable. Because of the efficient road network, the park can be visited with any type of vehicle throughout the year.

THE SEYCHELLES ISLANDS

Aldabra Atoll (16)

This is a natural reserve designated in 1982 as a "World Heritage Site." The reserve is a typical coral atoll (a ringlike coral island and reef that nearly or entirely encloses a lagoon) located north of the Mozambique Channel, 262 miles (420 km) northwest of Madagascar. It covers a total area of 135 sq. miles (350 sq. km).

The land animals of this reserve belong to about twenty different species, many of which are threatened by extinction.

Aldabra is noted for the presence of giant turtles, which number 152,000 specimens, and for important nesting areas of the green sea turtles. About one thousand female turtles come here to nest every year.

Among the native bird species, the park hosts a flightless bird which is limited to an area of 24 acres (100,000 sq. m) of coastal woodland. About 1,500 drongo birds inhabit this area.

Cousin Island (17)

This natural reserve of 66 acres (270,000 sq. m) stretches all the way to the ocean, about 1,300 feet (400 m) off the coast. It was acquired in 1968 by the International Council for Bird Preservation (ICBP). The Cousin Island reserve includes the nesting areas of three species of native birds threatened by extinction, including a warbler and a ringdove. Large colonies of seabirds as well as sea turtles also breed here. Visitors are allowed only during day hours. Only twenty visitors at a time are allowed, three times a week. No overnight accommodations are available.

Aride Island (18)

This natural reserve includes 172 acres (700,000 sq. m) of vegetation, consisting mainly of interesting native species. About one million pairs of seabirds nest here, such as tropic birds, terns, shearwaters and frigate birds.

MASCARENE

On Mauritius and nearby islands there are numerous parks and reserves, some private, others public. In March 1984 a treaty was signed between the government of Mauritius, the Jersey Wildlife Preservation Trust, and the International Council for Bird Preservation for implementing a nature research program on the island. Certain animal species which are now threatened by extinction are being bred here for later release to the wild.

Ile aux Serpents (19)

This natural reserve is located 16 miles (25 km) northeast of Cap Malheureux, the northernmost point of Mauritius. It is a small, volcanic island of 74 acres (300,000 sq. m) inhabited by bird colonies (about two million birds: sooty terns, blue-faced boobies, and noddy terns). There are also interesting native reptiles including geckos and skinks.

Round Island (20)

This is a nature reserve located about 15 miles 24 km) northeast of Cap Malheureux. It has a surface of about 0.5 sq. mile (1.6 sq. km).

This island (a former volcano) is important for the presence of a few native palm tree species that still grow in

A Kalahari Desert, winds often form violent swirls capable of lifting large amounts of sand and dust.

their natural state. Among the reptiles which inhabit the island four species are threatened by extinction: gecko, skink, and two types of boas. Quite a few colonies of seabirds nest here such as the stormy petrel.

This reserve covers a total area of 14 sq. miles (36 sq. km) and is located on the island of Mauritius. The reserve is important for the attempt to conserve parts of the original forest, which hosts a variety of plants (palms, orchids, and an amazing ibiscus). All of the most important birds of Mauritius are present in this reserve, such as hawks, white-eyes, and brown-eared bulbuls. Of particular interest is a colony of native fruit-eating bats.

Macchabee-Bel Ombre (21)

MADAGASCAR

In Madagascar there are numerous nature reserves, national parks and special reserves. Access to natural reserves is strictly limited to authorized researchers and scientists. Interested parties should contact: Service de Protection de la flore et de la faune et de gestion du patrimoine forestier, Direction des Eaux et Forets, Antananarivo. National parks and special reserves are instead open to tourists. Visitors, however, should obtain permits, which are issued by the above-mentioned Direction des Eaux et Forets.

Perinet/ Analamazaotra (22)

This reserve covers a total area of 3 sq. miles (8 sq. km) east of Moramanga. The reserve was established to protect the endrina lemur. The vegetation is of an Asian mountain type and is luxuriant with tree ferns, orchids, and various epiphytes. There are other notable species of lemurs besides the endrina, as well as birds, native invertebrate animals, civets, and mongooses.

Betampona (23)

This is reserve number 1. It covers an area of 8.5 sq. miles (22 sq. km) northwest of Toamasina (Tamatave). This reserve offers several interesting ecosystems typical of the low elevation area of the eastern domain. There are numerous springs and also portions of primary and secondary forests consisting of evergreen trees. Many species of lemurs live here, such as the endrina and the fork-marked lemur. There is a large population of birds and interesting native mongooses and civets.

Nosy Mangab (24)

This is a special reserve covering about 2 sq. miles (5 sq. km). It was established in 1965 with the purpose of saving the aye-aye, the rarest lemur in the world. Located on the island by the same name, east of Maroantsetra, it has a forest environment typical of the eastern coast with numerous palms and native ferns.

D'Ambre Mountain (25)

This park is located south of Antsiranana. Its 70 sq. miles (182 sq. km) of volcanic soil enclose a mountain forest typical of the eastern coast. Numerous crater lakes and spectacular waterfalls add to the beauty of this park, which is famous for its orchids, tree ferns, and epiphytic plants. It is also well-known for birds, reptiles, and certain rare species of lemurs.

Tsaratanana (26)

Reserve Number 4. With its 188 sq. miles (486 sq. km) this reserve surrounds Madagascar's highest mountain, the Maromokotra, which is 9,472 feet (2,887 m) high. The reserve is covered mostly by native mountain vegetation and is located southeast of Ambanja. In addition to primary and secondary evergreen forests, this area is known for its grasses and for its lichen growths. It is also famous for the great variety of orchids and for the presence of lemurs (including the macaco lemur), mongooses, civets, birds, and reptiles.

Isalo (27)

Located west of Ihosi, this national park encloses an area of 315 sq. miles (815 sq. km) surrounding the spectacular mountain range of the Isalo with its majestic canyons and steep slopes. Among native plant species is the Ravenea palm. A few species of lemurs, mongooses, civets, and native reptiles live in the park.

Tsimanampetsotsa (28)

Reserve Number 10. This reserve covers an area of 167 sq. miles (432 sq. km). It includes a lake and part of a forest on limestone soil. Its woodlands consist of drought-tolerant plants such as didiereas and spurges. The reserve is an important sanctuary for numerous species of aquatic and migratory birds. The common dwarf flamingo and various species of ducks can be found here. A rare native turtle also inhabits this area.

Berenty (29)

This is a small but important reserve established in the 1940s by the French family de Heaulme, which still owns it. It covers an area of about 1 sq. mile (2 sq. km) of forest on the banks of the Mandrare River in the Fort Dauphin region of southern Madagascar. The tamarind and hackberry are the

predominant trees of this reserve. The undergrowth consists of evergreen bushes. Heading inland, the forest becomes a woodland of drought-tolerant acacias and aloes. Further inland it becomes a desert with thorny didiereas.

There are quite a few ring-tailed and sifaka lemurs in addition to several species of nocturnal lemurs. There is a colony of lemurs descendant from a few animals that escaped captivity in 1974 following a hurricane.

The birds are represented by ground cuckoos, native vanga-shrikes, and two species of black parrots.

A small group of rare turtles is also being bred here with the purpose of reintroducing it into regions where it is presently endangered.

The de Heaulme family also owns a large plantation of agaves, which they have dedicated to scientific research.

The reserve has facilities for visitor tours.

Andohahela (30)

Located northwest of Fort Dauphin, nature reserve number 11 is famous for its plant variety. The plant species found in this reserve often display contrasting ecological requirements that can be found throughout the 293-square-mile (760 sq. km) area. There is a succession of primary and secondary evergreen forests as well as dry forests with spurges and didiereas. One can also spot a peculiar palm tree native to this region. Lemurs and well-distinguished bird species live in the different environments of this area.

Andringitra (31)

Nature reserve Number 5. This reserve is located south of Ambalavo. It covers an area of about 120 sq. miles (312 sq. km) in a mountainous region which includes the Andringitra Mountain. Here one of Andringitra's peaks (Pic Boby) reaches the second highest elevation in Madagascar—8,720 feet (2,658 m). In 1922 this peak was climbed by a French expedition headed by Perrier de la Bathie and Descarpentries. It is said that the dog belonging to the climbers was the first to reach the summit, which was named in its honor.

Numerous species of plants grow on the mountain, including heaths, spurges, grasses, and drought-tolerant plants. Animal life is represented by a few lemurs, by the small carnivorous fossa cat, and by several species of chameleons.

Preceding pages: The cattle-egret is one of the most common species of herons of both Madagascar and the tropics. This colony is found at Tamatave.

GLOSSARY

algae: primitive organisms which resemble plants but do not have true roots, stems, or leaves.

amphibian: any of a class of vertebrates that usually begins life in the water as a tadpole with gills and later develops lungs.

arboreal: of or like a tree; living in trees or adapted for living in trees.

arid: lacking enough water for things to grow; dry and barren.

botanist: a plant specialist. Botanists study the science of plants, which deals with the life, structure, growth, classification, etc. of a plant.

camouflage: a disguise or concealment of any kind.

carnivore: a meat-eating organism such as a predatory mammal, a bird of prey, or an insectivorous plant.

continent: one of the principal land masses of the earth. Africa, Antarctica, Asia, Europe, North America, South America, and Australia are regarded as continents.

deciduous forests: forests having trees that shed their leaves at a specific season or stage of growth.

dormant: live, but not actively growing; in a state of suspended animation.

ecology: the relationship between organisms and their environment.

ecosystem: a system made up of a community of animals, plants, and bacteria and its physical and chemical environment.

entomology: the branch of zoology that deals with insects.

environment: the circumstances or conditions of a plant or animal's surroundings.

epiphyte: a plant, such as certain orchids or ferns, that grows on another plant upon which it depends for physical support but not for nutrients.

erosion: natural processes such as weathering, abrasion, and corrosion, by which material is removed from the earth's surface.

evolution: a gradual process in which something changes into a different and usually more complex or better form.

genus: a classification of plants or animals with common distinguishing characteristics.

geology: the science dealing with the physical nature and history of the earth.

habitat: the areas or type of environment in which a person or other organism normally occurs.

insectivore: an animal that eats insects. The tenrecs of Madagascar are insectivores.

lichen: a primitive plant formed by the association of blue-green algae with fungi.

metamorphosis: a change in form, shape, structure, or substance as a result of development.

migrate: to move from one region to another with the change in seasons. Many animals have steady migration patterns.

naturalist: a person who studies nature, especially by direct observation of animals and plants.

niche: the specific space occupied by an organism within its habitat; a small space or hollow.

nocturnal: referring to animals that are active at night. Geckos and lemurs have nocturnal habits.

nomads: people without a permanent home, who move around constantly in search of food and pasture for their animals.

omnivore: an animal that eats both plants and other animals.

peninsula: a land area almost entirely surrounded by water and connected to the mainland by a narrow strip of earth called an isthmus.

plankton: microscopic plant and animal organisms which float or drift in the ocean or in bodies of fresh water. Plankton represent an important food source for many animals.

plumage: the feathers of a bird.

predator: an animal that lives by preying on others.

prey: an animal hunted or killed for food by another.

reptile: a cold-blooded vertebrate having lungs, a bony skeleton, and a body covered with scales or horny plates.

ruminant: cud-chewing animals; grazing animals having a stomach with four chambers.

savanna: a treeless plain or a grassland characterized by scattered trees, especially in tropical or subtropical regions having seasonal rains.

species: a distinct kind, sort, variety, or class. Plant and animal species have a high degree of similarity and can generally interbreed only among themselves.

steppe: a large plain having few trees. Many of the steppes in Europe, Asia, and Africa have been cultivated and planted with grain crops.

succulent: having thick, fleshy tissues for storing water. Bryophyllums and aloes are succulent plants.

temperate: a climate which is neither very cold nor very hot, but rather moderate.

topography: the accurate and detailed description of a place.

transpiration: the giving off of moisture through the surface of leaves and other parts of a plant.

valley: a stretch of low land lying between hills or mountains and usually having a river or stream flowing through it.

veld: open, grassy country in South Africa, with few bushes and almost no trees.

vertebrate: having a backbone or spinal column. Fishes, amphibians, reptiles, birds, and mammals are primarily vertebrates, having a segmented body or cartilaginous spinal column.

xerophyte: a plant structurally adapted to growing under very dry or desert conditions, often having smaller leaf surfaces for avoiding water loss, thick fleshy parts for water storage, and hair, spines, or thorns.

zoologist: a specialist in the study of animals; their life structure, growth, and classification.

INDEX

DATE DUE

DATE DUE

574.5   Daturi, Augusta
Dat

Southern Africa